P9-CRJ-998

greatest ever

indian

BARNES
& NOBLE
NEW YORK

This 2006 edition published by Barnes & Noble, Inc.,
by arrangement with Parragon Publishing.

Produced by THE BRIDGEWATER BOOK COMPANY

ISBN-13: 978-0-7607-9046-5
ISBN-10: 0-7607-9046-9

Printed and bound in Indonesia

3 5 7 9 10 8 6 4 2

NOTES FOR THE READER

• This book uses imperial, metric or US cup measurements. Follow the same units of measurement throughout; do not mix imperial and metric.
• All spoon measurements are level: teaspoons are assumed to be 5 ml, and tablespoons are assumed to be 15 ml.
• Unless otherwise stated, milk is assumed to be whole, eggs and individual vegetables such as carrots are medium, and pepper is freshly ground black pepper.
• Recipes using raw eggs should be avoided by infants, the elderly, pregnant women, convalescents, and anyone suffering from an illness.
• Do not use a larger quantity of herbs than is recommended in the recipes.

Contents

Introduction

Indian cuisine is among the most diverse and versatile in the world, employing a wide range of cooking techniques and a vast array of ingredients and flavors. This is hardly surprising given the sheer size of the country and its long and eventful history. The story of Indian food is, indeed, one of geography and history, but it is also profoundly influenced by religion, and these three elements are closely interwoven with one another.

Each region of India has its own specialties and characteristic dishes. For example, Mumbai, formerly Bombay, is famous for its pork curries, while Bengali cuisine features fish and Madras is well known for its superb vegetarian food. Nevertheless, in broad culinary terms the country can be divided into the north and south. The dishes of the north bear witness to a succession of invasions throughout the centuries, whereas foreign influences are less pronounced in the south. The Moguls left a heritage of finely prepared, creamy, and rich-tasting dishes, while India is indebted to the Persians for pilafs and many other rice dishes, and to the Portuguese for the introduction of vinegar, the defining ingredient of vindaloo curries. Portuguese and Spanish explorers were also responsible for introducing the chili to Asia from its native South America.

Only the British, it seems, had little effect on the country's cooking. However, so enamored were they of Indian seasonings and chutneys that they did much to spread the word of this delicious cuisine.

An abundance of fruit and vegetables grows in the south and, together with lentils and rice, features in the staple dishes of the region. The north is a wheat-growing area and a wide variety of different breads is produced. The main religion in southern India is Hinduism and so the majority of the population is vegetarian. There are many Hindus in the north too, but observance of a vegetarian diet is often less strict. Meat, mainly lamb and chicken, does feature in traditional dishes, although no Hindu would eat beef, because the cow is regarded as a sacred animal. In coastal areas, many Hindus eat fish, not classifying it as meat. Muslim communities eat all kinds of meat, apart from pork or products derived from pigs, which are thought to be unclean. Other groups who practise other religions are scattered throughout the country, whether Christians in the former Portuguese colony of Goa, Middle Eastern Jews, or Parsees, all of whom have their own dietary regulations and traditional foods.

Cooking techniques and equipment

One of the great things about Indian cooking is that it rarely requires much last-minute attention. It also needs little in the way of special equipment. Most Western kitchens will already include virtually everything you need to prepare the recipes in this book.

The proper blending of spices is an essential part of Indian cooking. Indian cooks grind fresh spices for each dish, using a stone rolling pin and flat stone called a sil and batta, or a heavy stone or cast-iron mortar and pestle called a hamal-dista. These are available from specialty shops, but you can use an ordinary mortar and pestle or spice grinder instead.

A heavy-bottom skillet is essential and, if you are keen on Balti dishes, you might want to invest in a karahi or Balti pan. Resembling a wok, this has a round base and two handles. A tava or tawa is a kind of grill pan used by Indian cooks for roasting spices and cooking chapatis and other flat breads. However, neither is essential if you have a good quality skillet.

Other specialty equipment includes a coconut grater, called a narial kas, and a fine strainer called a chalni. While it is fun to use authentic tools, an ordinary grater and strainer will serve the purpose.

The one piece of specialty equipment for which there is no Western equivalent is the tandoor, a clay or brick oven, which is popular in parts of northern India. Several tandoori recipes that have been adapted for cooking in a Western-style oven are included in this book.

Special ingredients

Asafetida

This is a pungent spice; its foul smell disappears on cooking and it adds a pleasant flavor to dishes. It is best bought ground and stored in an airtight container.

Ata flour

Also known as chapati flour, this is a whole-wheat flour widely used for making breads. Well sifted whole-wheat flour can be used instead.

Besan

Also known as gram flour, this is made from chickpeas. It is used to flavor and thicken curries and for making pakoras and bhajias.

Paneer

This smooth, white cheese with a delicate flavor is used throughout India by both vegetarians and meat eaters—it is often combined with meat. Ricotta cheese may be used instead.

Chana dal

A split yellow lentil with a slightly sweet taste, chana dal are used in a variety of vegetable dishes and as a binding agent.

Fenugreek

The fresh herb is used in a number of vegetable dishes and in some meat dishes. Always discard the stalks, which taste unpleasantly bitter, and use only the small leaves. Fenugreek seeds give curry spice mixes their strong aroma.

Ghee

Clarified butter or ghee used to be the standard cooking fat throughout India. Nowadays, vegetable ghee, often corn oil, is more popular because it contains less saturated fat.

Kalonji

Also known as nigella, these tiny black seeds have a slight peppery flavor and are used mainly in vegetable dishes.

Masoor dal

These split red lentils are widely available and are used in many dishes. They are actually orange in color and become much paler when they are cooked.

Moong dal

This split yellow lentil is quite similar to chana dal, but smaller.

Panch phoran

This is an Indian mix of five spices—cumin seeds, onion seeds, mustard seeds, fenugreek seeds, and anise.

Tamarind

Sour tasting and strongly flavored, this is the sticky, dried, dark brown pod of the tamarind plant. It has to be soaked in hot water, then strained before use. Tamarind paste is more convenient to use and is available in jars from Asian food stores. If unavailable, you can use lemon juice as a substitute.

Toor dal

This split lentil is similar to chana dal.

Urid dal

This lentil is available with its hull, which is black, and may be called black gram, or hulled, when it is creamy white. It takes quite a long time to cook.

Basic Recipes

curry paste

4 tbsp coriander seeds
2 tbsp cumin seeds
1 tbsp fenugreek seeds
1 tbsp fennel seeds
2 curry leaves
2 dried red chilies
2 tsp ground turmeric
2 tsp chili powder
5 tbsp white wine vinegar
2 tbsp water
½ cup vegetable oil, plus extra for sealing

1 Grind the coriander, cumin, fenugreek, and fennel seeds, curry leaves, and dried red chilies in a spice grinder or with a mortar and pestle. Transfer to a bowl and stir in the turmeric, chili powder, vinegar, and water to make a smooth paste.

2 Heat the vegetable oil in a large, heavy-bottom skillet, then add the paste and cook over low heat, stirring constantly, for 10 minutes, or until all the water has been absorbed and the oil rises to the surface.

3 Let cool, then spoon into a glass jar with a lid. To preserve the curry paste, heat a little more oil in a clean pan and pour it over the surface. Store in the refrigerator for up to 1 month.

garlic paste

4 oz/115 g garlic cloves, halved
½ cup water

1 Place the garlic cloves and water in a food processor or blender and process to make a paste. Transfer to a glass jar with a lid and store in the refrigerator for up to 1 month.

ginger paste

4 oz/115 g fresh gingerroot, coarsely chopped
½ cup water

1 Place the ginger and water in a food processor or blender and process to make a paste. Transfer to a glass jar with a lid and store in the refrigerator for up to 1 month.

garam masala

1 cinnamon stick
8 dried red chilies
5 tbsp coriander seeds
2 tbsp cumin seeds
2 tsp cardamom seeds
1 tsp fennel seeds
1 tsp black mustard seeds
2 tsp black peppercorns
1 tsp whole cloves

1 Dry-fry the cinnamon stick and dried red chilies in a heavy-bottom skillet over low heat, stirring constantly, for 2 minutes. Add the coriander, cumin, cardamom, fennel, and black mustard seeds, peppercorns, and cloves and dry-fry, stirring and shaking the skillet constantly, for 8 minutes, or until they give off their aroma.

2 Remove the skillet from the heat and let cool. Transfer the contents to a spice grinder and process until ground. Alternatively, use a mortar and pestle. Store in an airtight container in the refrigerator for up to 3 months.

Soups

All the soups in this chapter would make a delicious and substantial lunchtime snack, perhaps served with some Indian bread such as Naan Bread (see page 177), or as an imaginative start to a dinner party. They range from quite fiercely spiced soups, such as Spinach Soup (see page 10), to ones that are milder and more subtle in flavor, like Seafood Soup (see page 12). These soups are extremely easy to prepare and most can be made ahead of time, then reheated until piping hot just before serving.

spinach soup

serves six

2 tsp coriander seeds
2 tsp cumin seeds
1 tbsp ghee or vegetable oil
2 onions, chopped
1 tbsp Ginger Paste (see page 7)
2 tsp Garlic Paste (see page 7)
6 curry leaves, coarsely torn
2 dried red chilies, crushed
2 tsp black mustard seeds
½ tsp fenugreek seeds
1 tsp ground turmeric
1 cup masoor dal
2 potatoes, diced
5 cups vegetable stock
2 lb 4 oz/1 kg fresh spinach, tough stems removed, plus extra to garnish
2 tbsp lemon juice
1¼ cups coconut milk
salt and pepper

COOK'S TIP

You can prepare this soup the day before and when cool, cover and store in the refrigerator until required. Make sure that it is piping hot before serving.

1

2

1 Heat a heavy-bottom skillet and dry-fry the coriander and cumin seeds, stirring constantly, until they give off their aroma. Tip into a mortar and grind with a pestle. Alternatively, grind in a spice mill or blender.

2 Heat the ghee in a large pan. Add the onions, Ginger Paste, Garlic Paste, curry leaves, chilies, mustard seeds, and fenugreek seeds and cook over low heat, stirring frequently, for 8 minutes, or until the onions are softened and golden. Stir in the ground, dry-fried spices and turmeric and cook for an additional 1 minute. Add the masoor dal, potatoes, and stock and bring to a boil, then reduce the heat and simmer for 15 minutes, or until the potatoes are tender. Stir in the spinach and cook for 2–3 minutes, or until wilted.

3

3 Remove the pan from the heat and let cool slightly. Ladle the soup into a food processor or blender and process until smooth. Return to the pan and stir in the lemon juice and coconut milk and season to taste with salt and pepper. Reheat gently, stirring occasionally, but do not boil. Ladle into warmed soup bowls and garnish with fresh spinach leaves, then serve immediately.

seafood soup

serves four

1 cup vegetable stock
2 carrots, diced
3 garlic cloves, finely chopped
3 tbsp chopped cilantro,
plus extra to garnish
1 tsp cumin seeds
1 tsp black peppercorns
½-inch/1-cm piece fresh gingerroot,
chopped
1 tbsp ghee or vegetable oil
1 onion, chopped
1 fresh green chili, seeded
and chopped
1 potato, diced
2 tsp ground coriander
7 oz/200 g cooked shrimp, peeled
and deveined
generous ¼ cup plain yogurt
⅔ cup milk
3 tbsp dry white wine
8 scallops, shucked
salt and pepper

VARIATION

You could substitute 16 freshly cooked, shucked mussels for the scallops or 8 shucked oysters.

1 Pour the stock into a pan and add the carrots, 2 of the garlic cloves, the chopped cilantro, cumin seeds, peppercorns, and ginger. Bring to a boil, then cover and simmer for 20 minutes. Strain the stock into a pitcher and make up to 3 cups with water, if necessary.

2 Heat the ghee in a separate pan. Add the onion, chili, and remaining garlic and cook for 5 minutes. Add the potato and ground coriander and cook for 2 minutes. Add the reserved stock and bring to a boil, then cover and simmer for 5 minutes, or until the potato is tender.

3 Remove the pan from the heat and let cool slightly. Ladle the contents into a food processor, then add half the shrimp and process until smooth. Return the soup to the pan and add the remaining shrimp with the yogurt and milk. Reheat gently. Stir in the wine and scallops, then season to taste with salt and pepper and simmer for 2–3 minutes, or until the scallops are just cooked. Ladle into warmed bowls, and garnish with chopped cilantro, then serve.

lentil soup

serves four

4 cups water

generous 1 cup toor dal or chana dal

1 tsp paprika

½ tsp chili powder

½ tsp ground turmeric

2 tbsp ghee or vegetable oil

1 fresh green chili, seeded and finely chopped

1 tsp cumin seeds

3 curry leaves, coarsely torn

1 tsp sugar

salt

1 tsp Garam Masala (see page 7), to garnish

VARIATION

For a fuller flavor, cook the dal in vegetable stock instead of water.

1 Bring the water to a boil in a large, heavy-bottom pan. Add the dal, then cover and simmer, stirring occasionally, for 25 minutes.

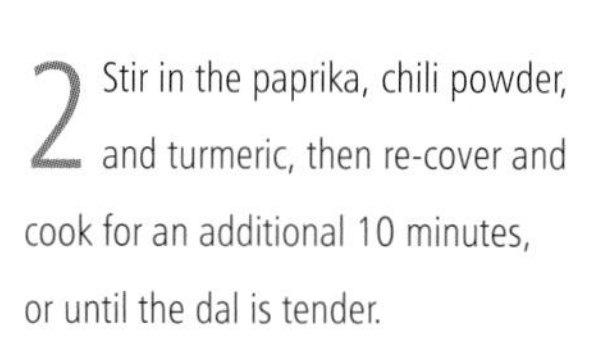

2 Stir in the paprika, chili powder, and turmeric, then re-cover and cook for an additional 10 minutes, or until the dal is tender.

3 Meanwhile, heat the ghee in a small skillet. Add the chili, cumin seeds, and curry leaves and cook, stirring constantly, for 1 minute.

4 Add the spice mixture to the dal. Stir in the sugar and season with salt to taste. Ladle into warmed soup bowls, then sprinkle with Garam Masala and serve immediately.

cauliflower soup

serves six

- 1 tbsp ghee or vegetable oil
- 1 small cauliflower, broken into florets
- 2 potatoes, diced
- 3 tbsp water
- 1 tsp Garlic Paste (see page 7)
- 1 tbsp Ginger Paste (see page 7)
- 2 tsp ground turmeric
- 1 tsp black mustard seeds
- 1 tsp cumin seeds
- 1 tbsp coriander seeds, lightly crushed
- 4 cups vegetable stock
- salt and pepper
- 1¼ cups plain yogurt

1 Heat the ghee in a large, heavy-bottom pan. Add the cauliflower, potatoes, and water and bring to a boil, then reduce the heat and simmer, covered, for 10 minutes.

2 Stir in the Garlic Paste, Ginger Paste, turmeric, mustard seeds, cumin seeds, and coriander seeds and cook, stirring frequently, for 3 minutes. Add the stock and season to taste with salt and pepper. Bring to a boil, then cover and simmer for 20 minutes.

3 Remove the pan from the heat and let cool slightly. Ladle the mixture into a food processor or blender and process until smooth. Return to the pan and stir in the yogurt. Reheat gently until piping hot. Taste and adjust the seasoning, if necessary, and serve immediately.

VARIATION

For a more subtle flavor and color, you can substitute ½ teaspoon of saffron threads for the ground turmeric.

pepper water soup

serves six

- 2 tbsp ghee or vegetable oil
- 2 dried red chilies
- 4 curry leaves, coarsely torn
- 1 tsp Garlic Paste (see page 7)
- 1 tsp cumin seeds
- ½ tsp ground turmeric
- ½ tsp mustard seeds
- pinch of asafetida
- salt and pepper
- 1¼ cups tomato juice
- 6 tbsp lemon juice
- ⅔ cup water
- chopped cilantro, to garnish

VARIATION

Poach 2 lb/900 g diced chicken in 2½ cups water until tender. Proceed as in main recipe, adding the chicken to reheat at the last moment.

1 Heat the ghee in a large, heavy-bottom pan. Add the chilies, curry leaves, Garlic Paste, cumin seeds, turmeric, mustard seeds, asafetida, and ½ teaspoon pepper. Cook over medium heat, stirring frequently, for 5–8 minutes, or until the chilies are charred.

2 Add the tomato juice, lemon juice, and water and season with salt to taste. Bring to a boil, then reduce the heat and simmer for 10 minutes.

3 Remove the chilies, then taste and adjust the seasoning, if necessary. Ladle into warmed soup bowls and sprinkle with chopped cilantro, then serve immediately.

Meat & Poultry

From kabobs to curries and from chicken to lamb, the choice is huge. There are richly flavored stews, quick stir-fries, colorful tandoori dishes, and succulent roasts. Whether you want an easy, but tasty, dish for a midweek family supper, or something special for entertaining guests, you are sure to find exactly the right recipe here.

Lamb is undoubtedly India's favorite meat, and this chapter includes such classics as Rogan Josh (see page 32) and Lamb Koftas (see page 20). However, both pork and beef also feature.

Chicken is also the perfect partner for subtle spices and is transformed when served, southern Indian-style, in a combination of coconut milk, lime juice, and cilantro. Favorites among the recipes here include Chicken Dhansak (see page 68).

lamb koftas

serves four

- 1 lb/450 g fresh ground lamb
- 1 small onion, finely chopped
- 1 tsp ground cumin
- 1 tsp ground coriander
- 1 tsp chili powder
- 1 tsp Garam Masala (see page 7)
- 1 tsp Garlic Paste (see page 7)
- 2 tbsp chopped cilantro
- salt
- generous ¾ cup vegetable oil
- 6 scallions, chopped
- 1 green bell pepper, seeded and chopped
- 1½ cups fava beans, thawed if frozen
- 12 baby corn cobs, thawed if frozen
- 1 small cauliflower, cut into florets
- 3 fresh green chilies, seeded and chopped
- 1 tbsp lime juice
- 1 tbsp fresh mint leaves

VARIATION

You can use any mixture of vegetables you have to hand, such as red bell pepper, broccoli, chopped green beans, or snow peas.

1 Place the lamb, onion, cumin, ground coriander, chili powder, Garam Masala, Garlic Paste, and half the cilantro in a bowl and mix well with your hands. Season with salt to taste. Cover and let chill in the refrigerator for a few minutes.

2 Heat 3 tablespoons of the vegetable oil in a preheated wok or large skillet. Add the scallions and cook, stirring frequently, for 1 minute. Add the green bell pepper, fava beans, corn cobs, cauliflower, and chilies and cook over high heat, stirring, for 3 minutes, or until crisp-tender. Reserve.

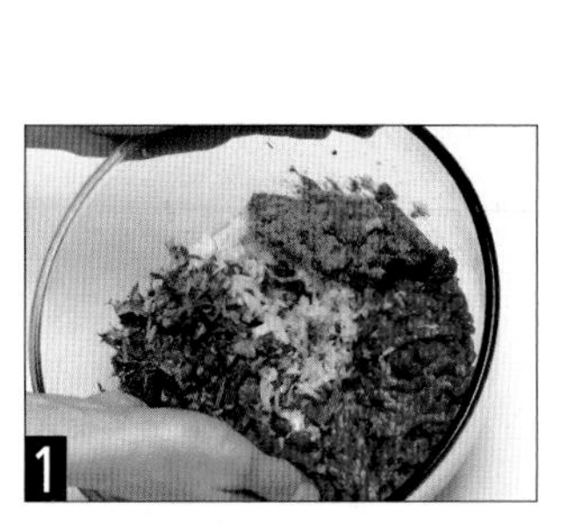

1

2

3 Heat the remaining vegetable oil in a separate preheated wok or large skillet. Meanwhile, form the lamb mixture into small balls or ovals between the palms of your hands. Add the koftas, in batches, to the hot oil and cook, turning them frequently, until golden brown. Remove with a slotted spoon and drain on paper towels. When they are all cooked, return the vegetables to the heat and stir in the koftas. Cook over low heat, stirring frequently, for 5 minutes, or until heated through. Sprinkle with the lime juice and serve garnished with the remaining cilantro and mint leaves.

COOK'S TIP

The lamb must be finely ground for making koftas. If necessary, process in a food processor for 1 minute before mixing with the other ingredients.

3

hot spicy lamb in sauce

serves six–eight

¾ cup vegetable oil
2 lb 4 oz/1 kg lean leg of lamb, cut into large pieces
1 tbsp Garam Masala (see page 7)
5 onions, chopped
⅔ cup yogurt
2 tbsp tomato paste
2 tsp finely chopped fresh gingerroot
2 garlic cloves, crushed
1½ tsp salt
2 tsp chili powder
1 tbsp ground coriander
2 tsp ground nutmeg
3¾ cups water
1 tbsp ground fennel seeds
1 tbsp paprika
1 tbsp besan
3 bay leaves
1 tbsp all-purpose flour
2 tbsp warm water
2–3 fresh green chilies, chopped
cilantro, chopped, plus extra to garnish
thin slivers of fresh gingerroot, to garnish

1 Heat the oil in a skillet. Add the meat and half of the Garam Masala and stir-fry for 7–10 minutes, or until the meat is well coated. Using a slotted spoon, remove the meat and reserve until required.

2 Add the onions to the skillet and cook until golden brown. Return the meat to the skillet, then reduce the heat and let simmer, stirring occasionally.

3 Mix the yogurt, tomato paste, ginger, garlic, salt, chili powder, ground coriander, nutmeg, and the rest of the Garam Masala together in a separate bowl. Pour this mixture over the meat and stir-fry, mixing the spices well into the meat, for 5–7 minutes.

4 Stir in half the water, then add the fennel, paprika, and besan. Add the remaining water and the bay leaves, then reduce the heat. Cover and cook for 1 hour, stirring occasionally.

5 Mix the all-purpose flour and warm water together, then pour over the curry. Sprinkle with the chilies and chopped cilantro and cook until the meat is tender and the sauce thickens. Garnish with ginger and extra chopped cilantro and serve.

broiled ground lamb

serves four

5 tbsp vegetable oil
2 onions, sliced
1 lb/450 g fresh ground lamb
2 tbsp yogurt
1 tsp chili powder
1 tsp finely chopped fresh gingerroot
1 garlic clove, crushed
1 tsp salt
1½ tsp Garam Masala (see page 7)
½ tsp ground allspice
2 fresh green chilies
1 bunch of cilantro

TO GARNISH
1 onion, cut into rings
chopped cilantro
1 lemon, cut into wedges

TO SERVE
Naan Bread (see page 177)
salad greens

1 Preheat the broiler to medium. Heat the oil in a pan. Add the onions and cook until golden brown.

2 Place the ground lamb in a large bowl. Add the yogurt, chili powder, ginger, garlic, salt, Garam Masala, and allspice and mix well.

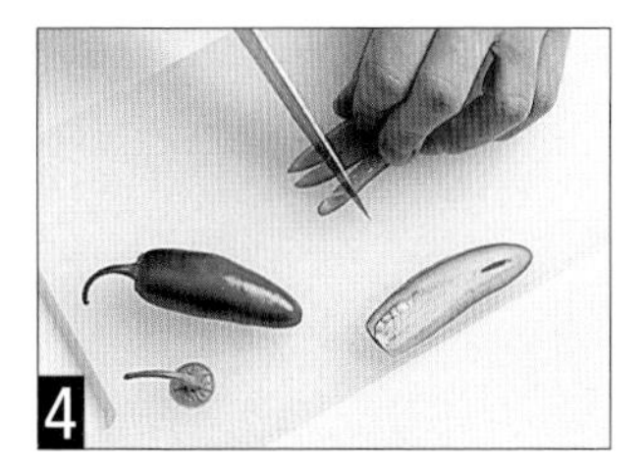

3 Add the lamb mixture to the fried onions and stir-fry for 10–15 minutes. Remove the pan from the heat and reserve.

4 Meanwhile, seed the chilies, then place in a food processor with half of the cilantro and process until finely chopped. Alternatively, finely chop the chilies and cilantro with a sharp knife. Reserve.

5 Place the lamb mixture in a food processor and process until smooth. Alternatively, place in a large bowl and mash with a fork. Mix the lamb mixture with the reserved chilies and cilantro and blend well.

6 Transfer the mixture to a shallow heatproof dish. Cook under the hot broiler for 10–15 minutes, moving the mixture about with a fork. Watch it carefully to prevent it burning.

7 Garnish with onion rings, cilantro, and lemon wedges and serve with Naan Bread and salad.

lamb keema

serves four

2 tbsp ghee (see page 164) or vegetable oil
1 onion, chopped
1 cinnamon stick
4 cardamom pods, lightly crushed
1 curry leaf
4 cloves
1 tsp Ginger Paste (see page 7)
1 tsp Garlic Paste (see page 7)
1 lb/450 g fresh ground lamb
2 tsp ground coriander
2 tsp ground cumin
1 tsp chili powder
⅔ cup plain yogurt
1 tbsp dried fenugreek
salt
chopped cilantro, to garnish

COOK'S TIP

In India, this dish would be flavored with fresh fenugreek leaves, known as *methi*. You would need 1 bunch of fresh leaves. Always remove and discard the bitter stems.

1 Heat the ghee in a karahi, preheated wok, or large, heavy-bottom pan. Add the onion and cook over low heat, stirring occasionally, for 5 minutes, or until softened.

2 Add the cinnamon stick, cardamoms, curry leaf, and cloves and cook, stirring constantly, for 1 minute, then add the Ginger Paste and Garlic Paste and cook, stirring constantly, for an additional 1 minute.

3 Add the ground lamb and sprinkle over the ground coriander, cumin, and chili powder. Cook for 5 minutes, or until the lamb is lightly browned, stirring and breaking up the meat with a wooden spoon.

4 Stir in the yogurt and fenugreek and season with salt to taste. Cover and cook over low heat for 20–30 minutes, or until the lamb is tender and the liquid has been absorbed. Ladle into a warmed serving dish and discard the curry leaf. Garnish with chopped cilantro and serve.

VARIATION

You could add 1 cup frozen peas 10 minutes before the end of the cooking time, if you like.

lamb curry in a thick sauce

serves six

2 lb 4 oz/1 kg lean lamb
7 tbsp plain yogurt
½ cup almonds
2 tsp Garam Masala (see page 7)
2 tsp finely chopped fresh gingerroot
2 garlic cloves, crushed
1½ tsp chili powder
1½ tsp salt
1¼ cups vegetable oil
3 onions, finely chopped
4 green cardamoms
2 bay leaves
3 fresh green chilies, chopped
2 tbsp lemon juice
2 cups canned tomatoes
1¼ cups water
1 small bunch of cilantro, chopped
freshly cooked rice, to serve

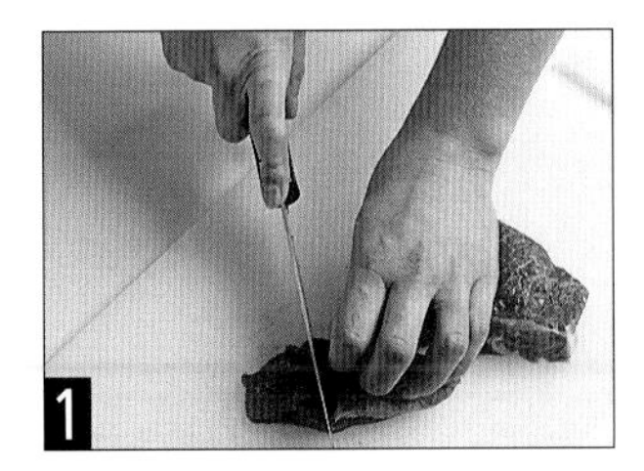

1 Using a sharp knife, cut the lamb into small, even-size pieces.

2 Mix the yogurt, almonds, Garam Masala, ginger, garlic, chili powder, and salt together in a large bowl. Stir until well mixed.

3 Heat the oil in a large pan. Add the onions, cardamoms, and bay leaves and stir-fry until golden brown.

4 Add the meat and yogurt mixture to the pan and stir-fry for 3–5 minutes.

5 Add 2 of the green chilies, the lemon juice, and canned tomatoes to the mixture in the pan and stir-fry for an additional 5 minutes.

6 Add the water, then cover and let simmer over low heat for 35–40 minutes.

7 Add the remaining green chili and cilantro and stir until the sauce has thickened. Remove the lid and increase the heat if the sauce is too watery.

8 Transfer the curry to warmed serving plates and serve hot with freshly cooked rice.

marinated roast lamb

serves six

1¾ cups plain yogurt
½ cup lemon juice
3 tbsp malt vinegar
2 tsp chili powder
2 tsp Ginger Paste (see page 7)
2 tsp Garlic Paste (see page 7)
1 tsp brown sugar
1 tsp salt
few drops red food coloring (optional)
5 lb 8 oz/2.5 kg leg of lamb
vegetable oil, for brushing
cilantro sprigs, to garnish

COOK'S TIP

Red food coloring gives the lamb an attractive appearance. However, some synthetic coloring agents have been associated with allergies and other effects, so you may wish to omit it.

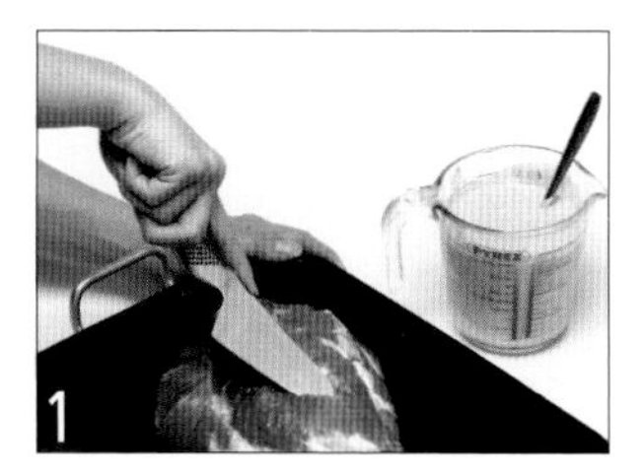

1

1 Mix the yogurt, lemon juice, vinegar, chili powder, Ginger Paste, Garlic Paste, sugar, salt, and food coloring (if using) together in a bowl. Make several deep gashes all over the lamb and place in a large roasting pan. Pour over the yogurt mixture, turning to coat and pressing it well into the gashes. Cover and let chill in the refrigerator for 8 hours or overnight.

2 Preheat the oven to 375°F/190°C. Remove the lamb from the refrigerator and bring to room temperature. Roast the lamb in the preheated oven for 1¼ hours, basting occasionally with the marinade.

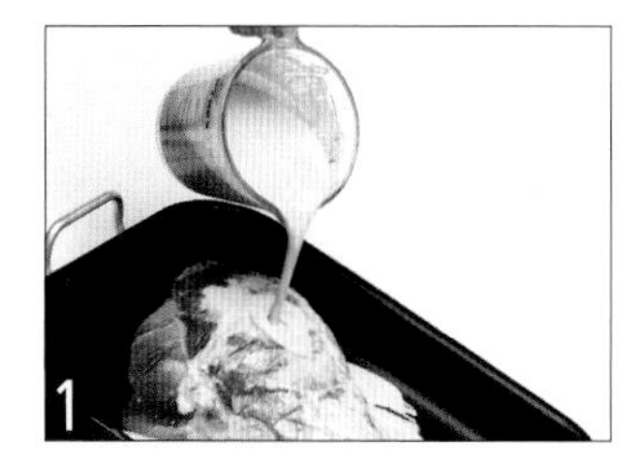

1

3

3 Remove the lamb from the oven and reduce the oven temperature to 325°F/160°C. Place the lamb on a large sheet of foil and brush with vegetable oil, then wrap the foil around the meat to enclose it completely. Return to the oven and roast for an additional 45–60 minutes, or until tender.

4 Let the lamb rest for 10 minutes before carving and serving, garnished with a few cilantro sprigs.

cauliflower with meat

serves four

1 cauliflower
2 fresh green chilies
1¼ cups vegetable oil
2 onions, sliced
1 lb/450 g lean cubed lamb
1½ tsp finely chopped fresh gingerroot
1–2 garlic cloves, crushed
1 tsp chili powder
1 tsp salt
1 small bunch of cilantro, chopped
3¾ cups water
1 tbsp lemon juice

BAGHAAR
⅔ cup vegetable oil
4 dried red chilies
1 tsp mixed mustard and onion seeds

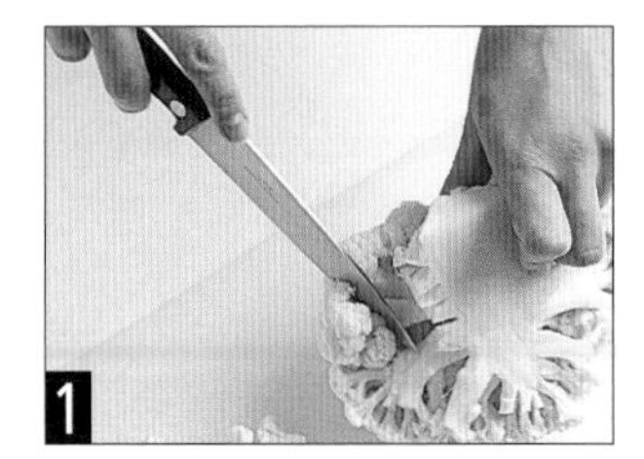

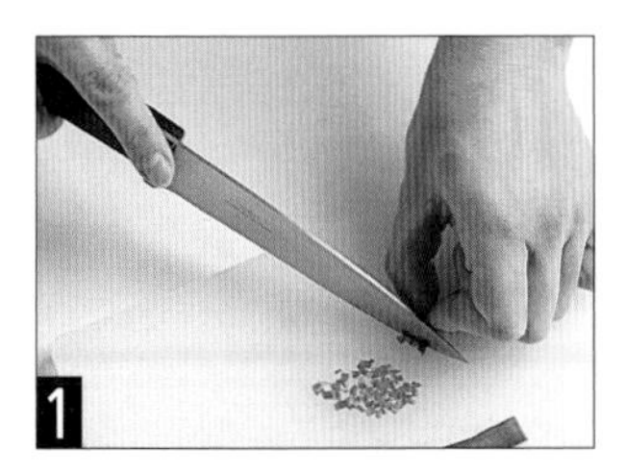

1 Using a sharp knife, cut the cauliflower into small florets. Chop the green chilies finely.

2 Heat the oil in a large skillet. Add the onions and cook until golden brown. Reduce the heat and add the meat, stirring.

3 Add the ginger, garlic, chili powder, and salt. Stir-fry for 5 minutes, stirring to mix.

4 Add half of the green chili and half of the cilantro. Stir in the water, then cover and cook over low heat for 30 minutes.

5 Add the cauliflower and simmer for 15–20 minutes, or until the water has evaporated completely. Stir-fry the mixture for an additional 5 minutes. Remove the skillet from the heat and sprinkle over the lemon juice.

6 To make the baghaar, heat the oil in a small pan. Add the dried red chilies and the mixed mustard and onion seeds and cook until they turn a darker color, stirring occasionally. Remove the pan from the heat and pour the mixture over the cauliflower.

7 Garnish with the remaining green chili and chopped cilantro. Serve immediately.

ground lamb with peas

serves four

- 6 tbsp vegetable oil
- 1 onion, sliced
- 2 fresh red chilies, chopped
- 1 bunch of cilantro, chopped
- 2 tomatoes, chopped
- 1 tsp salt
- 1 tsp finely chopped fresh gingerroot
- 1 garlic clove, crushed
- 1 tsp chili powder
- 1 lb/450 g fresh lean ground lamb
- 1 cup peas
- 2 fresh green chilies, to garnish

1 Heat the oil in a medium-size pan. Add the onion slices and cook until golden brown, stirring.

2 Add the red chilies, half of the chopped cilantro, and the tomatoes to the pan and reduce the heat to a simmer.

3 Add the salt, ginger, garlic, and chili powder to the mixture in the pan and stir well.

4 Add the ground lamb to the pan and stir-fry the mixture for 7–10 minutes.

5 Add the peas and cook for an additional 3–4 minutes, stirring occasionally.

6 Transfer the lamb and pea mixture to warmed serving plates and garnish with green chilies and the remaining cilantro.

COOK'S TIP

The flavor of garlic varies in strength depending on how it is prepared. A whole garlic clove added to a dish will give it the flavor but not the pungency of garlic; a halved clove will add a little "bite"; a finely chopped garlic clove will release most of its flavor, and a crushed clove will release all of the flavor.

1

2

3

lamb pot roast

serves four

5 lb 8 oz/2.5 kg leg of lamb
2 tsp chopped fresh gingerroot
2 tsp crushed garlic
2 tsp Garam Masala (see page 7)
1 tsp salt
2 tsp black cumin seeds
4 black peppercorns
3 cloves
1 tsp chili powder
3 tbsp lemon juice
1¼ cups vegetable oil
1 large onion, peeled but kept whole
about 9 cups water
TO SERVE
salad greens
freshly cooked potatoes

COOK'S TIP

Traditionally, a pan called a *degchi* is used for pot-roasting in India. It is set over hot ashes and contains hot coals in its lid.

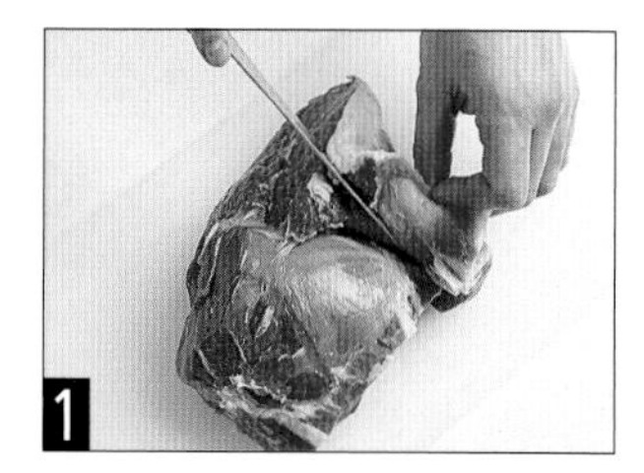

1 Using a sharp knife, remove the fat from the lamb. Prick the lamb all over with a fork.

2 Mix the ginger, garlic, Garam Masala, salt, black cumin seeds, peppercorns, cloves, and chili powder together in a bowl. Stir in the lemon juice and mix well. Spoon the mixture over the leg of lamb and rub into the meat, making sure it is well coated, then reserve.

3 Heat the oil in a large pan. Add the meat and place the onion alongside the leg of lamb.

4 Add enough water to cover the meat and cook over low heat for 2½–3 hours, turning occasionally. (If the water has evaporated after a while and the meat is not tender, add a little extra water.) Once the water has completely evaporated, turn the roast over to brown it on all sides.

5 Transfer the roast to a serving dish. Cut the roast into slices or serve it whole to be carved at the table. Serve the lamb hot or cold with salad greens and potatoes.

rogan josh

serves six

1 cup plain yogurt
½ tsp cayenne pepper
¼ tsp asafetida
2 lb 4 oz/1 kg diced lamb
1 tbsp coriander seeds
1 tbsp cardamom seeds
1 tsp cumin seeds
1 tsp white poppy seeds
8 black peppercorns
4 cloves
1¼-inch/3-cm piece fresh gingerroot
4 garlic cloves
2 tbsp almonds
1¼ cups water
4 tbsp ghee or vegetable oil
1 onion, chopped
1 tsp ground turmeric
2 tbsp chopped cilantro
1 tsp Garam Masala (see page 7)
salt

1 Mix the yogurt, cayenne, and asafetida together in a large, shallow dish. Add the lamb and toss well to coat. Cover and reserve.

2 Preheat the oven to 275°F/140°C. Place the coriander seeds and the cardamom, cumin, and poppy seeds in a food processor or blender with the peppercorns, cloves, ginger, garlic, almonds, and 4 tablespoons of the water and process to make a paste, adding a little more water, if necessary. Reserve until required.

3 Heat the ghee in a flameproof casserole. Add the onion and cook over low heat for 10 minutes, or until golden. Stir in the spice paste and turmeric and cook, stirring, for 5 minutes. Add the lamb, with its marinade, then increase the heat to high and cook, stirring, for 10 minutes. Reduce the heat, then cover and simmer for 45 minutes.

4 Stir 4 tablespoons of the water into the casserole and cook, stirring, until it has been incorporated. Stir in another 4 tablespoons of the water and cook until incorporated. Add the remaining water, then re-cover the casserole and simmer for 15 minutes. Stir the chopped cilantro and Garam Masala into the lamb and season with salt to taste. Cover, then transfer the casserole to the oven and cook for an additional 25 minutes. Serve immediately.

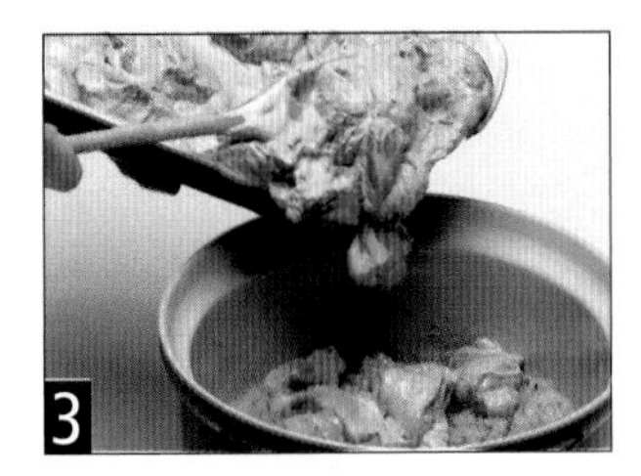
3

1

4

meatballs in sauce

serves four

1 lb/450 g fresh ground lamb
1 tsp crushed fresh gingerroot
1 garlic clove, crushed
1 tsp Garam Masala (see page 7)
1½ tsp poppy seeds
1 tsp salt
½ tsp chili powder
1 onion, finely chopped
1 fresh green chili, finely chopped
¼ bunch of cilantro, finely chopped
1 tbsp besan
⅔ cup vegetable oil

SAUCE
2 tbsp vegetable oil
3 onions, finely chopped
2 small cinnamon sticks
2 large black cardamoms
1 tsp finely chopped fresh gingerroot
1 garlic clove, crushed
1 tsp salt
generous ¼ cup plain yogurt
⅔ cup water

TO GARNISH
finely chopped cilantro
1 fresh green chili, finely chopped
1 lemon, cut into wedges

1 Place the lamb in a large bowl. Add the ginger, garlic, Garam Masala, poppy seeds, salt, chili powder, onion, chili, cilantro, and besan and mix well with a fork.

2 With dampened hands, form the mixture into small meatballs and reserve.

3 To make the sauce, heat the oil in a skillet. Add the onions and cook until golden brown. Add the cinnamon sticks and cardamoms, then reduce the heat and stir-fry for an additional 5 minutes. Add the ginger, garlic, salt, yogurt, and water and stir to mix well.

4 Transfer to a serving bowl and garnish with the chopped cilantro and chili.

5 Heat the oil in a pan. Add the meatballs and cook, turning occasionally, for 8–10 minutes, or until golden brown.

6 Transfer the meatballs to warmed serving plates and garnish with lemon wedges. Serve with the sauce.

potatoes cooked with meat & yogurt

serves six

3 potatoes
1¼ cups vegetable oil
3 onions, sliced
2 lb 4 oz/1 kg leg of lamb, cubed
1 tsp Garam Masala (see page 7)
1½ tsp finely chopped fresh gingerroot
1–2 garlic cloves, crushed
1 tsp chili powder
3 black peppercorns
3 green cardamoms
1 tsp black cumin seeds
2 cinnamon sticks
1 tsp paprika
1½ tsp salt
⅔ cup plain yogurt
2½ cups water
TO GARNISH
2 fresh green chilies, chopped
chopped cilantro

1 Peel and cut each potato into 6 pieces.

2 Heat the oil in a pan. Add the sliced onions and cook until golden brown. Remove the onions from the pan and reserve.

3 Add the meat to the pan with the Garam Masala and stir-fry for 5–7 minutes over low heat.

4 Add the onions and remove the pan from the heat.

5 Mix the ginger, garlic, chili powder, peppercorns, cardamoms, cumin seeds, cinnamon sticks, paprika, and salt together in a small bowl. Add the yogurt and mix well.

6 Return the pan to the heat and gradually add the spice and yogurt mixture. Stir-fry for 7–10 minutes. Add the water, then reduce the heat and cook, covered, for 40 minutes, stirring occasionally.

7 Add the potatoes to the pan and cook, covered, for an additional 15 minutes, gently stirring the mixture occasionally. Garnish with green chilies and cilantro and serve immediately.

6

3

4

shish kabobs

serves two

1 lb/450 g fresh lean ground lamb

1 tsp meat tenderizer

¼ bunch of cilantro

1 onion, finely chopped

2 fresh green chilies, finely chopped

2 tbsp plain yogurt

1 tsp finely chopped fresh gingerroot

1 garlic clove, crushed

1 tsp ground cumin

1 tsp ground coriander

½ tsp salt

1 tsp chili powder, plus extra to garnish

½ tsp ground allspice

1 tsp Garam Masala (see page 7)

TO SERVE

1 lemon, cut into wedges

Raita (see page 222)

1 Place the lamb in a bowl, then add the meat tenderizer and mix in well. Reserve for at least 3 hours.

2 Preheat the broiler to medium. Finely chop the cilantro. Mix the onion, green chilies, and cilantro together in a bowl.

3 Mix the yogurt, ginger, garlic, ground cumin, ground coriander, salt, chili powder, allspice, and Garam Masala together in a separate bowl. Blend with the onion mixture.

4 Add the combined mixture to the lamb and mix together. Divide the mixture into 10–12 equal portions. Roll 2 portions around each metal skewer with your fingers, pressing all around.

VARIATION

Serve in pita bread for great party food. The cooked meat can also be chopped into a salad.

5 Broil the kabobs under the hot broiler for 8–10 minutes, turning and basting occasionally with oil.

6 Sprinkle with chili powder and serve with lemon wedges and a Raita of your choice.

tomatoes cooked with meat & yogurt

serves two–four

- 1 tsp Garam Masala (see page 7)
- 1 tsp finely chopped fresh gingerroot
- 1 garlic clove, crushed
- 2 black cardamoms
- 1 tsp chili powder
- ½ tsp black cumin seeds
- 2 x 1-inch/2.5-cm cinnamon sticks
- 1 tsp salt
- ⅔ cup plain yogurt
- 1 lb 2 oz/500 g lean cubed lamb
- ⅔ cup vegetable oil
- 2 onions, sliced
- 2½ cups water
- 2 large tomatoes, cut into fourths
- 2 tbsp lemon juice
- 2 fresh green chilies, chopped, to garnish

1 Mix the Garam Masala, ginger, garlic, cardamoms, chili powder, black cumin seeds, cinnamon sticks, salt, and yogurt together in a large bowl.

COOK'S TIP

Kormas are slowly braised dishes, many of which are the rich and spicy, Persian-inspired Mogul dishes served on special occasions. Yogurt is often featured, both as a marinade and as the cooking liquid.

2 Add the meat to the yogurt and spice mixture and mix until the meat is well coated. Reserve.

3 Heat the oil in a large skillet. Add the onions and cook until golden brown.

4 Add the meat and stir-fry for 5 minutes. Reduce the heat and add the water, then cover and simmer for 1 hour, stirring occasionally.

5 Add the tomatoes to the curry and sprinkle with the lemon juice. Let the curry simmer for an additional 7–10 minutes.

6 Garnish the curry with chopped chilies and serve hot.

lean lamb cooked in spinach

serves two–four

1¼ cups oil
2 onions, sliced
¼ bunch of cilantro, chopped
3 fresh green chilies, chopped
1½ tsp finely chopped fresh gingerroot
1–2 garlic cloves, crushed
1 tsp chili powder
½ tsp ground turmeric
1 lb/450 g lean cubed lamb
1 tsp salt
2 lb 4 oz/1 kg fresh spinach leaves, chopped or 15 oz/425 g canned spinach
scant 3 cups water
TO GARNISH
fresh gingerroot, shredded
chopped cilantro

1 Heat the oil in a skillet. Add the onions and cook until they turn a pale golden color.

2 Add the cilantro and two-thirds of the chopped green chilies to the skillet and stir-fry for 3–5 minutes.

3 Reduce the heat and add the ginger, garlic, chili powder, and turmeric to the mixture in the skillet. Stir well.

4 Add the lamb and stir-fry for 5 minutes. Add the salt and the spinach and cook, stirring occasionally, for an additional 3–5 minutes.

2

3

4

5 Add the water, stirring, then cover the skillet and cook over low heat for 45 minutes. Remove the lid and check the meat. If it is not tender, turn the meat over, then increase the heat and cook, uncovered, until the surplus water has been absorbed. Stir-fry the mixture for an additional 5–7 minutes.

6 Transfer the lamb and spinach mixture to a warmed serving dish and garnish with shredded ginger, cilantro, and the remaining chopped chili. Serve hot.

meat-coated eggs

serves six

1 lb/450 g fresh lean ground lamb
1 small onion, finely chopped
1 fresh green chili, finely chopped
1 tsp finely chopped fresh gingerroot
1 garlic clove, crushed
1 tsp ground coriander
1 tsp Garam Masala (see page 7)
1 tsp salt
1½ tbsp besan
7 eggs, 1 beaten and 6 hard-cooked and shelled
corn oil, for deep-frying
salad greens, to serve

TO GARNISH
tomato slices
1 lemon, cut into wedges

1 Place the lamb, onion, and chili in a bowl and mix together. Transfer the mixture to a food processor and process until well ground. Alternatively, grind by hand using a pestle and mortar.

2 Remove the mixture from the food processor and add the ginger, garlic, ground coriander, Garam Masala, salt, besan, and the beaten egg. Work the mixture together with your hands until well mixed.

3 Divide the mixture into 6 equal-size portions. Roll each portion out to form a flat circle, ¼ inch/5 mm thick. Place a hard-cooked egg in the center of each round and wrap the meat mixture around the egg to enclose it completely. When all 6 eggs have been covered, let stand in a cool place for 20–30 minutes.

VARIATION

You can serve these in a sauce. Use the recipe for Meatballs in Sauce (see page 34).

4 Meanwhile, heat the oil for deep-frying in a deep skillet to 350°F/180°C, or until a cube of bread browns in 30 seconds. Gently drop the coated eggs into the oil and deep-fry for 2–4 minutes, or until golden. Using a slotted spoon, remove the eggs from the oil and transfer to paper towels to drain. Garnish with tomato slices and lemon wedges and serve with salad.

1

2

3

spicy lamb chops

serves four–six

- 2 lb 4 oz/1 kg lamb chops
- 2 tsp finely chopped fresh gingerroot
- 2 garlic cloves, crushed
- 1 tsp pepper
- 1 tsp Garam Masala (see page 7)
- 1 tsp black cumin seeds
- 1½ tsp salt
- 3¾ cups water
- 2 eggs
- 1¼ cups oil

TO GARNISH

- Potato Wafers (see page 153)
- tomatoes
- 1 lemon, cut into wedges

1 Using a sharp knife, trim away any excess fat from the lamb chops.

2 Mix the ginger, garlic, pepper, Garam Masala, cumin seeds, and salt together in a bowl and rub all over the chops.

3 Bring the water to a boil in a pan. Add the chops and spice mixture and cook for 45 minutes, stirring occasionally. Once the water has evaporated, remove from the heat and let cool.

4 Using a fork, beat the eggs together in a large bowl.

5 Heat the oil in a large pan. Dip each lamb chop into the beaten egg and cook them in the oil for 3 minutes, turning once.

6 Transfer the chops to a large, warmed serving dish and garnish with Potato Wafers, tomatoes, and lemon wedges. Serve hot.

lamb & lentils

serves six

scant ½ cup chana dal
scant ½ cup masoor dal
scant ½ cup moong dal
scant ½ cup urid dal
generous ⅓ cup porridge oats
KORMA
3 lb 5 oz/1.5 kg cubed lamb
generous ¾ cup plain yogurt
2 tsp finely chopped fresh gingerroot
2 garlic cloves, crushed
1 tbsp Garam Masala (see page 7)
2 tsp chili powder
½ tsp ground turmeric
3 green cardamoms
2 cinnamon sticks
1 tsp black cumin seeds
2 tsp salt
1¾ cups oil
5 onions, sliced
scant 3 cups water
2 fresh green chilies
1 small bunch of cilantro, chopped
½ bunch of cilantro, chopped, to garnish

1 Soak the lentils and oats overnight. Drain and boil in a pan of water for 1–1 ½ hours, or until soft. Mash and reserve.

2 Place the lamb in a large bowl. Add the yogurt, ginger, garlic, Garam Masala, chili powder, turmeric, cardamoms, cinnamon sticks, cumin seeds, and salt; then mix and reserve.

3 Heat 1¼ cups of the oil in a pan. Add four-fifths of the onions and cook until golden. Add the meat and stir-fry for 7–10 minutes. Stir in the water, then reduce the heat and cook, covered, for 1 hour, stirring occasionally. If the meat is still not tender, add more water and cook for 15–20 minutes. Remove the pan from the heat.

4 Add the lentils to the meat, then stir and mix. If the mixture is too thick, add 1¼ cups water and stir, then cook for an additional 10–12 minutes. Add the chilies and cilantro. Transfer to a serving dish and keep warm.

5 Heat the remaining oil and cook the remaining onion until golden. Pour over the lamb and lentils. Garnish with chopped cilantro and serve.

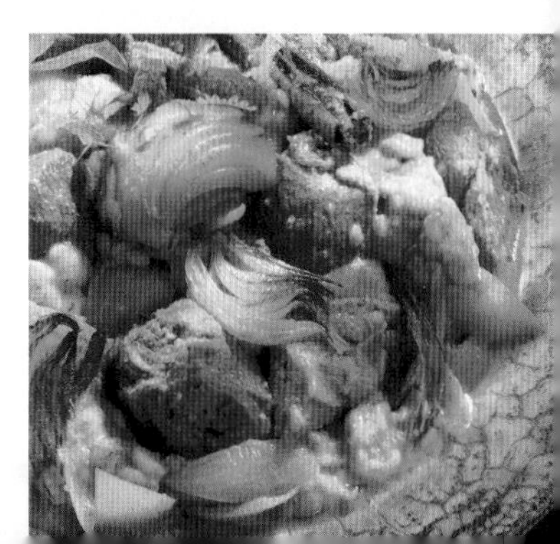

stuffed tomatoes

serves six

6 large firm tomatoes
scant ¼ cup unsalted butter
5 tbsp vegetable oil
1 onion, finely chopped
1 tsp finely chopped fresh gingerroot
1 garlic clove, crushed
1 tsp pepper
1 tsp salt
½ tsp Garam Masala (see page 7)
1 lb/450 g fresh ground lamb
1 fresh green chili
1 small bunch of cilantro, chopped
1 lemon, cut into wedges, to garnish
salad greens, to serve

VARIATION

You could use the same mixture to stuff red or green bell peppers, if you prefer.

1 Preheat the oven to 350°F/180°C. Rinse the tomatoes, then cut off the tops and scoop out the flesh.

2 Grease an ovenproof dish with the butter. Place the tomatoes in the dish.

3 Heat the oil in a pan. Add the onion and cook until golden.

4 Reduce the heat and add the ginger, garlic, pepper, salt, and Garam Masala. Stir-fry the mixture for 3–5 minutes.

5 Add the lamb to the pan and cook for 10–15 minutes.

6 Add the chili and cilantro and continue stir-frying the mixture for 3–5 minutes.

7 Spoon the lamb mixture into the tomatoes and replace the tops. Cook the tomatoes in the preheated oven for 15–20 minutes.

8 Transfer the tomatoes to serving plates, then garnish with lemon wedges and serve with salad greens.

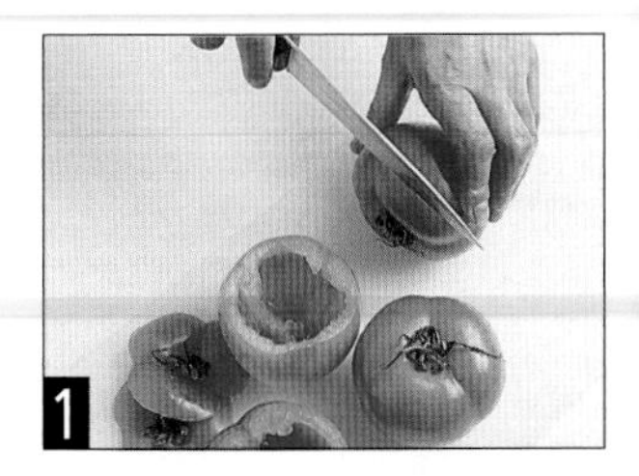
1

4

5

lamb with onions & dried mango powder

serves four

4 onions
1¼ cups vegetable oil
1 tsp finely chopped fresh gingerroot
1 garlic clove, crushed
1 tsp chili powder
pinch of ground turmeric
1 tsp salt
3 fresh green chilies, chopped
1 lb/450 g lean cubed lamb
2½ cups water
1½ tsp amchoor (dried mango powder)
1 small bunch of cilantro, chopped
freshly cooked rice, to serve

1 Using a sharp knife, chop 3 onions finely.

2 Heat ⅔ cup of the oil in a skillet. Add the onions and cook until golden brown. Reduce the heat and add the ginger, garlic, chili powder, turmeric, and salt. Stir-fry the mixture for 5 minutes, then add two-thirds of the chili.

3 Add the cubed lamb to the skillet and stir-fry the mixture for an additional 7 minutes.

4 Add the water, then cover and cook over low heat for 35–45 minutes, stirring occasionally, until the lamb is tender.

5 Meanwhile, slice the remaining onion. Heat the remaining oil in a skillet. Add the onion and cook until golden. Reserve.

6 Once the lamb is tender, add the amchoor, the remaining green chili, and chopped cilantro and stir-fry for 3–5 minutes.

7 Transfer the curry to a serving dish and pour the fried onion slices and oil along the center. Serve hot with freshly cooked rice.

cubed lamb kabobs

serves six–eight

2 lb 4 oz/1 kg lean lamb, boned and cubed
1 tsp meat tenderizer
1½ tsp finely chopped fresh gingerroot
1–2 garlic cloves, crushed
1 tsp chili powder
½ tsp ground turmeric
½ tsp salt
2 tbsp water
8 tomatoes, cut in half
8 small pickling onions
10 mushrooms
1 green bell pepper, cut into large pieces
1 red bell pepper, cut into large pieces
2 tbsp vegetable oil
2 lemons, cut into wedges, to garnish
TO SERVE
freshly cooked rice
Raita (see page 222)

1 Place the meat in a bowl, then sprinkle over the tenderizer and rub it in, using your hands. Let stand for 3 hours at room temperature.

2 Preheat the broiler to medium. Mix the ginger, garlic, chili powder, turmeric, and salt together in a bowl. Add the water and mix to form a paste. Add the meat and mix until it is well coated with the spices.

3 Thread the meat cubes onto metal skewers, alternating with the tomatoes, pickling onions, mushrooms, and bell peppers. Brush the meat and vegetables with the oil.

4 Grill the kabobs under the hot broiler for 25–30 minutes, or until the meat is cooked through. When cooked, remove the kabobs from the broiler and transfer to a serving plate. Arrange lemon wedges on the side and serve immediately with freshly cooked rice and a Raita of your choice.

2

2

3

spicy lamb curry in sauce

serves four

2 tsp cumin seeds
2 tsp coriander seeds
2 tsp dry unsweetened coconut
1 tsp mixed mustard and onion seeds
2 tsp sesame seeds
1 tsp finely chopped fresh gingerroot
1 garlic clove, crushed
1 tsp chili powder
1 tsp salt
1 lb/450 g lean cubed lamb
1¼ cups vegetable oil
3 onions, sliced
3¾ cups water
2 tbsp lemon juice
4 fresh green chilies, split
TO SERVE
Onion Dal (see page 158)
freshly cooked rice

1 Dry-roast the cumin and coriander seeds, the dry unsweetened coconut, mixed mustard and onion seeds, and the sesame seeds in a heavy-bottom skillet, shaking the skillet frequently to stop the spices from burning. Grind the roasted spices using a pestle and mortar.

2 Mix the roasted ground spices, ginger, garlic, chili powder, salt, and the cubed lamb together in a bowl. Reserve.

3 Heat 1¼ cups of the oil in a pan. Add the onions and cook until golden brown.

4 Add the meat mixture to the onions and stir-fry for 5–7 minutes over low heat. Add the water and simmer for 45 minutes, stirring occasionally. When the meat is cooked through, remove the pan from the heat and sprinkle with the lemon juice.

5 Heat the remaining oil in a separate pan. Add the split green chilies, then reduce the heat and cover with a lid. Remove the pan from the heat after 30 seconds and let cool.

6 Pour the chili-oil mixture over the lamb curry and serve hot with Onion Dal and freshly cooked rice.

2

2

3

pork with tamarind

serves six

2 oz/55 g dried tamarind, chopped
2 cups boiling water
2 fresh green chilies, seeded and coarsely chopped
2 onions, coarsely chopped
2 garlic cloves, coarsely chopped
1 lemongrass stem, bulb end coarsely chopped
2 tbsp ghee or vegetable oil
1 tbsp ground coriander
1 tsp ground turmeric
1 tsp ground cardamom
1 tsp chili powder
1 tsp Ginger Paste (see page 7)
1 cinnamon stick
2 lb 4 oz/1 kg diced pork fillet
1 tbsp chopped cilantro
Naan Bread (see page 177), to serve
TO GARNISH
cilantro sprigs
sliced fresh red chilies

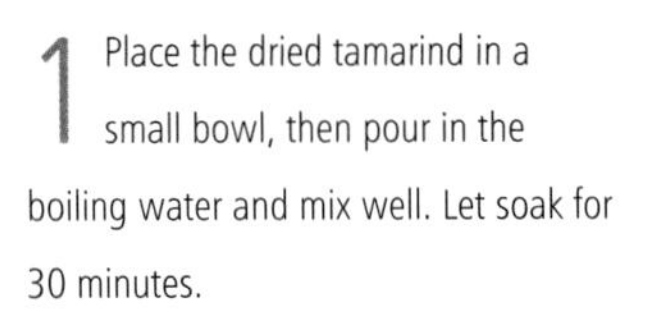

1 Place the dried tamarind in a small bowl, then pour in the boiling water and mix well. Let soak for 30 minutes.

2 Strain the soaking liquid into a clean bowl, pressing down the pulp with the back of a wooden spoon. Discard the pulp. Pour 1 tablespoon of the tamarind liquid into a food processor and add the green chilies, onions, garlic, and lemongrass and process until smooth.

3 Heat the ghee in a large, heavy-bottom pan. Add the ground coriander, turmeric, cardamom, chili powder, Ginger Paste, cinnamon stick, and the chili and onion paste, then cook, stirring, for 2 minutes, or until the spices give off their aroma.

4 Add the pork and cook, stirring constantly, until lightly browned and well coated in the spice mixture. Pour in the remaining tamarind liquid and bring to a boil, then reduce the heat and simmer, covered, for about 30 minutes. Remove the lid from the pan and simmer for an additional 30 minutes, or until the pork is tender. Stir in the chopped cilantro. Garnish with cilantro sprigs and sliced red chilies and serve with Naan Bread.

COOK'S TIP

Dried tamarind is usually sold in compressed blocks from large supermarkets and Asian food stores. If you can't find it, substitute 1¾ cups lemon juice, but remember that the flavor will not be the same.

pork & mushroom curry

serves four

1 lb 10 oz/750 g leg or shoulder of pork
3 tbsp vegetable oil
2 onions, sliced
2 garlic cloves, crushed
1-inch/2.5-cm piece fresh gingerroot, finely chopped
2 fresh green chilies, seeded and chopped, or 1–2 tsp dried chili flakes
1½ tbsp medium curry paste
1 tsp ground coriander
1½–2¼ cups thickly sliced mushrooms
3¾ cups chicken or vegetable stock
3 tomatoes, chopped
½–1 tsp salt
2 oz/55 g creamed coconut, chopped
2 tbsp ground almonds
freshly cooked rice, to serve
TO GARNISH
2 tbsp vegetable oil
1 green or red bell pepper, seeded and cut into thin strips
6 scallions, sliced
1 tsp cumin seeds

1 Cut the pork into small bite-size pieces. Heat the oil in a skillet. Add the pork, in batches, and cook until sealed, stirring frequently. Remove each batch of pork from the skillet as it is ready.

2 Add the onions, garlic, ginger, chilies, curry paste, and ground coriander to the skillet and cook gently for 2 minutes. Stir in the mushrooms, stock, and tomatoes, and season with a little salt to taste.

3 Return the pork to the skillet, then cover and simmer very gently for 1¼–1½ hours, or until the pork is tender.

1

2

4 Stir the creamed coconut and ground almonds into the curry. Cover and cook gently for 3 minutes.

5 Meanwhile, make the garnish. Heat the oil in a separate skillet. Add the bell pepper strips and scallion slices and cook gently until glistening and tender but still crisp. Stir in the cumin seeds and cook gently for 30 seconds. Spoon the mixture over the curry and serve immediately with freshly cooked rice.

2

pork with cinnamon & fenugreek

serves four

1 tsp ground coriander
1 tsp ground cumin
1 tsp chili powder
1 tbsp dried fenugreek
1 tsp ground fenugreek
⅔ cup plain yogurt
1 lb/450 g diced pork fillet
4 tbsp ghee or vegetable oil
1 large onion, sliced
2-inch/5-cm piece fresh gingerroot, finely chopped
4 garlic cloves, finely chopped
1 cinnamon stick
6 cardamom pods
6 whole cloves
2 bay leaves
¾ cup water
salt
Bombay Potatoes (see page 204), to serve

1 Mix the ground coriander, cumin, chilli powder, dried fenugreek, ground fenugreek, and yogurt together in a small bowl. Place the diced pork in a large, shallow, nonmetallic dish and add the spice mixture, turning well to coat. Cover and let marinate in the refrigerator for 30 minutes.

2 Heat the ghee in a large, heavy-bottom pan. Add the onion and cook, stirring occasionally, for 5 minutes, or until softened. Add the ginger, garlic, cinnamon stick, cardamom, cloves, and bay leaves and cook, stirring constantly, for 2 minutes, or until the spices give off their aroma. Add the meat with its marinade and the water, and season with salt to taste. Bring to a boil, then reduce the heat and simmer, covered, for 30 minutes.

3 Transfer the meat to a preheated wok or large, heavy-bottom skillet and cook over low heat, stirring constantly, until dry and tender. If necessary, occasionally sprinkle with a little water to prevent it sticking to the wok. Serve with Bombay Potatoes.

beef dhansak

serves six

2 tbsp ghee or vegetable oil
2 onions, chopped
3 garlic cloves, finely chopped
2 tsp ground coriander
2 tsp ground cumin
2 tsp Garam Masala (see page 7)
1 tsp ground turmeric
1 lb/450 g zucchini, peeled and chopped, or bitter gourd or pumpkin, peeled, seeded, and chopped
1 eggplant, peeled and chopped
4 curry leaves
generous 1 cup masoor dal
4 cups water
salt
2 lb 4 oz/1 kg stewing or braising steak, diced
cilantro leaves, to garnish

1 Heat the ghee in a large, heavy-bottom pan. Add the onions and garlic and cook over low heat, stirring occasionally, for 8–10 minutes, or until light golden. Stir in the ground coriander, cumin, Garam Masala, and turmeric and cook, stirring constantly, for 2 minutes.

2 Add the zucchini, eggplant, curry leaves, masoor dal, and water. Bring to a boil, then reduce the heat and simmer, covered, for 30 minutes, or until the vegetables are tender. Remove the pan from the heat and let cool slightly. Transfer the mixture to a food processor, in batches if necessary, and process until smooth. Return the mixture to the pan and season with salt to taste.

COOK'S TIP

Bitter gourds are widely used in Indian cooking. To prepare this long, knobbly vegetable, use a sharp knife to peel the ridged skin, then scrape out and discard the seeds before chopping.

3 Add the steak to the pan and bring to a boil. Reduce the heat, then cover and simmer for 1½ hours. Remove the lid and continue to simmer for an additional 30 minutes, or until the sauce is thick and the steak is tender. Serve garnished with cilantro leaves.

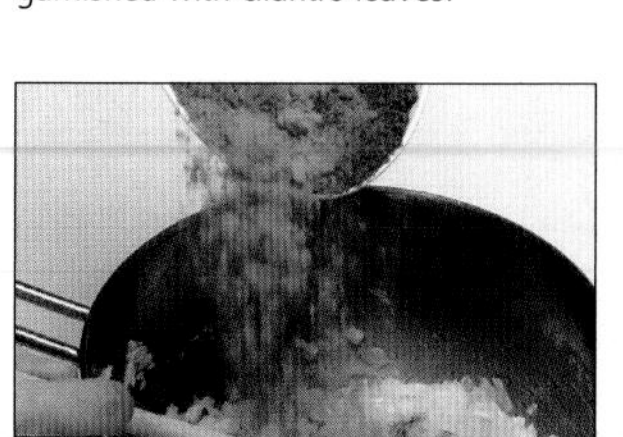
1

2

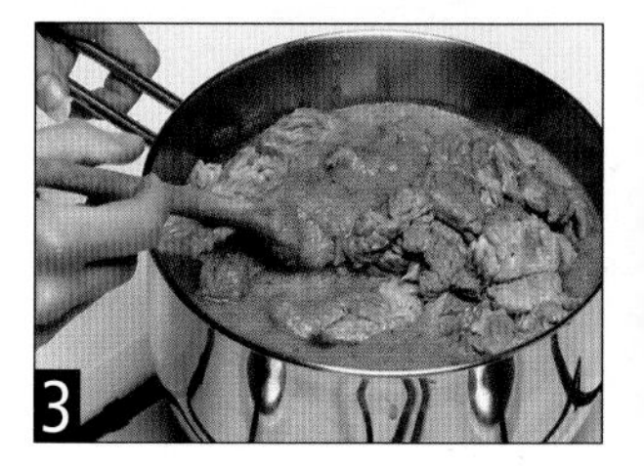
3

beef patties

serves four

3 tbsp chana dal
1 lb/450 g lean cubed beef
1 tsp finely chopped fresh gingerroot
1 garlic clove, crushed
1 tsp chili powder
1½ tsp salt
1½ tsp Garam Masala (see page 7)
3 fresh green chilies, chopped
1 bunch of cilantro
1 onion, chopped
1¼ cups vegetable oil
3¾ cups water
2 tbsp plain yogurt
1 egg

TO GARNISH
1 small onion, sliced into rings
1 lemon, cut into wedges

1 Rinse the chana dal twice under cold running water, removing any stones or other impurities. Boil in a pan of water until the water has been absorbed and the chana dal has softened. Place in a food processor and process to a paste.

2

3

3

2 Mix the beef, ginger, garlic, chili powder, salt, and Garam Masala in a bowl. Add about 2 of the green chilies, half of the cilantro, and the onion.

3 Heat 2 tablespoons of the oil in a pan. Add the meat mixture and water, then cover and cook over low heat for 45–60 minutes. Once the meat is tender, evaporate any excess water by removing the lid and cooking for an additional 10–15 minutes. Place the meat mixture in a food processor and process to a paste.

4 Place the yogurt, egg, chana dal paste, the remaining green chili, and cilantro in a bowl with the meat mixture and mix together with your fingers. Break off small balls of the meat paste and make 10–12 small, flat, circular shapes between the palms of your hands.

5 Heat the remaining oil in a skillet. Add the patties, in batches of 3, and cook for 5–10 minutes, turning once.

6 Serve garnished with onion rings and lemon wedges.

beef korma with almonds

serves six

1¼ cups vegetable oil
3 onions, finely chopped
2 lb 4 oz/1 kg lean cubed beef
1½ tsp Garam Masala (see page 7)
1½ tsp ground coriander
1½ tsp chopped fresh gingerroot
1–2 garlic cloves, crushed
1 tsp salt
⅔ cup plain yogurt
2 cloves
3 green cardamoms
4 black peppercorns
2½ cups water
pappadams, to serve
TO GARNISH
6 almonds, soaked, peeled, and chopped
2 fresh green chilies, chopped
chopped cilantro

1 Heat the oil in a large skillet. Add the onions and stir-fry until golden brown. Remove half of the onions from the skillet and reserve until required.

2 Add the meat to the remaining onions in the skillet and stir-fry for 5 minutes. Remove the skillet from the heat.

3 Mix the Garam Masala, ground coriander, ginger, garlic, salt, and yogurt together in a bowl. Gradually add the meat to the yogurt and spice mixture and mix until the meat is well coated. Add the meat mixture to the onions in the skillet, then return to the heat and stir for 5–7 minutes, or until the mixture is nearly brown in color.

4 Add the cloves, cardamoms, and peppercorns. Add the water, then reduce the heat and let simmer, covered, for 45–60 minutes. If the water has completely evaporated but the meat is still not tender enough, add another 1¼ cups water and cook for an additional 10–15 minutes, stirring occasionally.

5 Just before serving, garnish with the reserved onions, chopped almonds, chopped chilies, and cilantro. Serve with pappadams.

2

3

4

dry beef curry with carrot sambal

serves six

4 tbsp ghee or vegetable oil
2 fresh green chilies, seeded and chopped
2 onions, chopped
2 lb 4 oz/1 kg stewing or braising steak, diced
1 cup canned tomatoes, drained
salt
2 tsp ground coriander
1½ tsp Garam Masala (see page 7)
1 tsp ground cumin
3 tbsp Curry Paste (see page 7)
1¼ cups coconut milk
1 tbsp chopped cilantro, to garnish

CARROT SAMBAL
1 tbsp ghee or vegetable oil
1½ oz/40 g shredded coconut
1 tbsp black mustard seeds
1¾ cups grated carrots
4 tbsp lemon juice
scant ½ cup golden raisins
4 tbsp chopped fresh mint

1 To make the sambal, heat the ghee in a small skillet. Add the coconut and mustard seeds and cook over low heat, stirring constantly, for 2 minutes, or until the coconut is beginning to brown. Transfer the mixture to a bowl and stir in the carrots, lemon juice, golden raisins, and mint. Mix well and reserve.

2 To make the curry, heat the ghee in a large, heavy-bottom pan. Add the chilies and onions and cook over low heat, stirring occasionally, until the onions are light golden. Add the steak and cook, stirring frequently, for 10 minutes, or until browned all over. Stir in the tomatoes and season with salt to taste.

3 Mix the ground coriander, 1 teaspoon of the Garam Masala, the cumin, Curry Paste, and coconut milk together in a bowl, then add to the pan. Stir well, then half cover and simmer over low heat for 1½ hours. Remove the lid from the pan and continue to simmer for an additional 30 minutes, or until the meat is tender and the sauce is very thick. If it dries out too much, add a little water. Transfer to a warmed serving dish, then sprinkle with the remaining Garam Masala and chopped cilantro and serve with the carrot sambal.

1

2

3

sliced beef with yogurt & spices

serves four

1 lb/450 g lean beef, cut into 1-inch/2.5-cm slices
5 tbsp yogurt
1 tsp finely chopped fresh gingerroot
1 garlic clove, crushed
1 tsp chili powder
pinch of ground turmeric
2 tsp Garam Masala (see page 7)
1 tsp salt
2 cardamoms
1 tsp black cumin seeds
½ cup ground almonds
1 tbsp dry unsweetened coconut
1 tbsp poppy seeds
1 tbsp sesame seeds
1¼ cups vegetable oil
2 onions, finely chopped
1¼ cups water
TO GARNISH
2 fresh green chilies, cut into strips
chopped cilantro

1 Place the beef in a large bowl. Add the yogurt, ginger, garlic, chili powder, turmeric, Garam Masala, salt, cardamoms, and cumin seeds and mix together. Reserve.

2 Dry-roast the ground almonds, dry unsweetened coconut, poppy seeds, and sesame seeds in a heavy-bottom skillet until golden, shaking the skillet frequently to stop the spices from burning.

3 Transfer the spice mixture to a food processor and process until finely ground. Add 1 tablespoon of water to blend if necessary. Add the ground spices to the meat mixture and mix well.

4 Heat a little of the oil in a large pan. Add the onions and cook until golden brown. Remove the onions from the pan. Add the remaining oil and stir-fry the meat for 5 minutes, then return the onions to the pan and stir-fry for an additional 5–7 minutes. Add the water and let simmer over low heat, covered, for 25–30 minutes, stirring occasionally. Garnish with the strips of chili and cilantro and serve hot.

VARIATION

Substitute lamb for the beef in this recipe, if you prefer.

1

2

3

beef cooked in whole spices

serves four

1¼ cups vegetable oil
3 onions, finely chopped
1-inch/2.5-cm piece fresh gingerroot, shredded
4 garlic cloves, shredded
2 cinnamon sticks
3 green cardamoms
3 cloves
4 black peppercorns
6 dried red chilies
⅔ cup plain yogurt
1 lb/450 g lean cubed beef
3 fresh green chilies, chopped
2½ cups water

VARIATION

Replace the fresh green chilies with red ones, if you prefer.

1 Heat the oil in a skillet. Add the onions and cook, stirring, until golden brown.

2 Reduce the heat and add the ginger, garlic, cinnamon sticks, green cardamoms, cloves, black peppercorns, and red chilies and stir-fry for 5 minutes.

3 Place the yogurt in a bowl and whisk with a fork. Add the yogurt to the onions and stir well.

4 Add the meat and two-thirds of the chilies to the skillet and stir-fry the mixture for 5–7 minutes.

5 Gradually add the water to the skillet, stirring well. Cover and cook the beef and spice mixture for 1 hour, stirring and adding more water if necessary.

6 When thoroughly cooked through, remove the skillet from the heat and transfer the beef and spice mixture to a serving dish. Garnish with the remaining chopped chili.

2

3

4

classic vindaloo

serves six

⅔ cup malt vinegar
2 tbsp coriander seeds
1 tbsp cumin seeds
2 tsp chili powder
2 tsp ground turmeric
1 tsp cardamom seeds
2-inch/5-cm piece fresh gingerroot, coarsely chopped
4 garlic cloves, coarsely chopped
6 black peppercorns
6 whole cloves
1 cinnamon stick
salt
2 lb 4 oz/1 kg pork fillet, diced
6 curry leaves
3 tbsp ghee or vegetable oil
1 tsp black mustard seeds
⅔ cup water
freshly cooked rice, to serve

1 Place the vinegar, coriander, cumin, chili powder, turmeric, cardamom, ginger, garlic, peppercorns, cloves, cinnamon, and a pinch of salt in a food processor or blender and process to make a paste, adding a little more vinegar if necessary. Place the pork in a large, shallow, nonmetallic dish and pour over the spice paste, turning the meat to coat all over. Cover with plastic wrap and let marinate in the refrigerator for 1 hour. Arrange the curry leaves on top of the pork, then re-cover and let marinate for at least 8 hours or overnight.

2 Heat the ghee in a large, heavy-bottom pan. Add the mustard seeds and cook over low heat, stirring frequently, until they begin to splutter and give off their aroma. Add the pork, with the marinade, and the water. Bring to a boil, stirring constantly, then reduce the heat and simmer, covered, for 30 minutes.

3 Remove the lid from the pan and stir the curry. Simmer for an additional 30 minutes, or until the pork is tender. Transfer to a warmed serving dish and serve with rice.

1

1

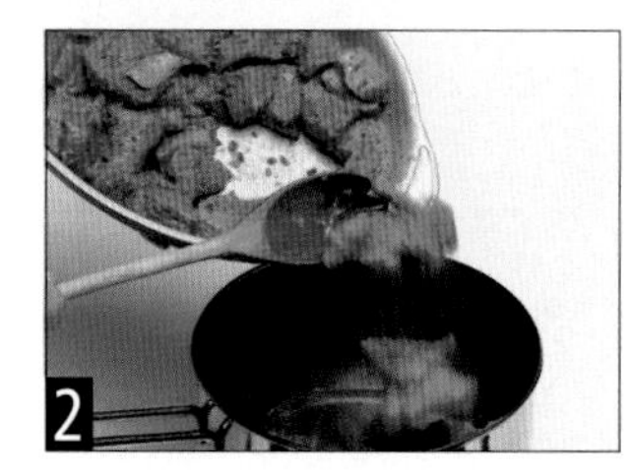

2

VARIATION

Serve with yellow rice: stir a pinch of ground turmeric with 1 tablespoon of boiling water until dissolved, then stir into the cooked rice until mixed.

COOK'S TIP

Remove the marinating meat from the refrigerator 30 minutes before you intend to begin cooking to bring it to room temperature.

chicken tikka

serves six

1 tsp finely chopped fresh gingerroot
1 garlic clove, crushed
½ tsp ground coriander
½ tsp ground cumin
1 tsp chili powder
3 tbsp plain yogurt
1 tsp salt
2 tbsp lemon juice
few drops of red food coloring (optional)
1 tbsp tomato paste
3 lb 5 oz/1.5 kg skinless, boneless chicken breasts
1 onion, sliced
3 tbsp vegetable oil
6 lettuce leaves
1 lemon, cut into wedges, to garnish

1 Blend the ginger, garlic, ground coriander, ground cumin, and chili powder together in a large bowl.

2 Add the yogurt, salt, lemon juice, red food coloring (if using), and the tomato paste to the spice mixture.

3 Using a sharp knife, cut the chicken into pieces. Add the chicken to the spice mixture and toss to coat well. Let marinate in the refrigerator for at least 3 hours, preferably overnight.

4 Preheat the broiler. Arrange the onion in the base of a flameproof dish. Carefully drizzle half of the oil over the onions.

5 Arrange the marinated chicken pieces on top of the onions and cook under the hot broiler, turning once and basting with the remaining oil, for 25–30 minutes.

6 Serve the chicken tikka on a bed of lettuce and garnish with the lemon wedges.

2

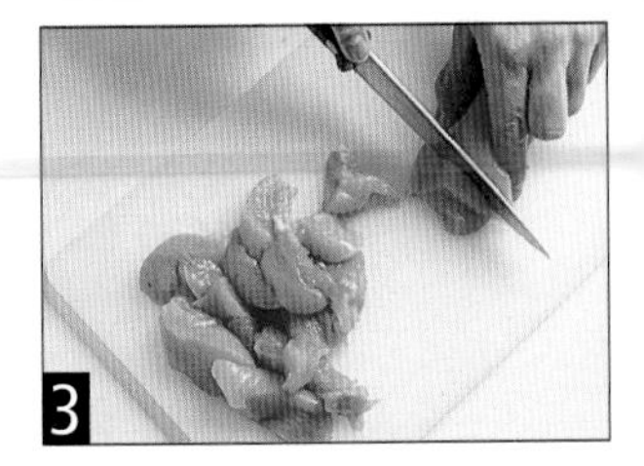
3

3

COOK'S TIP

Chicken Tikka can be served with Naan Bread (see page 177), Raita (see page 222), and Mango Chutney (see page 226), or as an appetizer.

chicken with spinach

serves four

8 oz/225 g fresh spinach leaves, rinsed
1 fresh green chili, seeded and chopped
1 tbsp chopped fresh gingerroot
2 garlic cloves, chopped
4 tbsp water
2 tbsp ghee or vegetable oil
8 black peppercorns
1 bay leaf
1 onion, finely chopped
1 cup canned tomatoes, drained
1 tsp chili powder
1 tbsp Curry Paste (see page 7)
salt
⅔ cup chicken stock or water
4 tbsp plain yogurt, plus extra to garnish
8 skinless chicken thighs

1 Place the spinach in a large pan with just the water clinging to the leaves after rinsing, then cover and cook for 4–5 minutes, or until wilted. Transfer to a food processor or blender and add the green chili, ginger, garlic, and water. Process until smooth.

2 Heat the ghee in a karahi or pan. Add the peppercorns and bay leaf and cook over low heat, stirring constantly, for 1–2 minutes, or until they give off their aroma. Add the onion and cook, stirring occasionally, for 10 minutes, or until golden. Add the tomatoes and cook for 2 minutes, breaking them up with a wooden spoon. Add the chili powder and Curry Paste and season with salt to taste. Cook, stirring constantly, for 2 minutes.

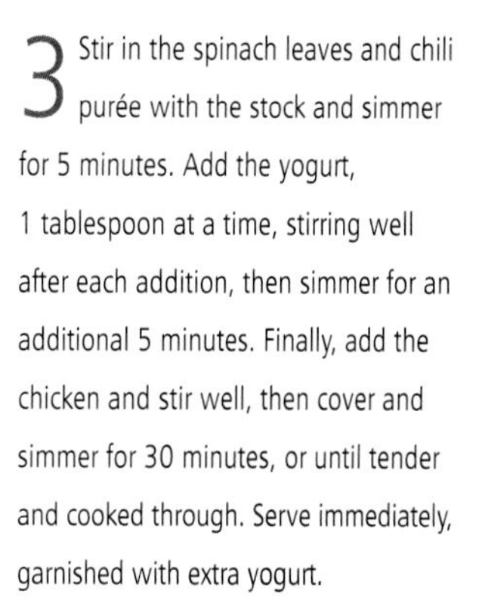

3 Stir in the spinach leaves and chili purée with the stock and simmer for 5 minutes. Add the yogurt, 1 tablespoon at a time, stirring well after each addition, then simmer for an additional 5 minutes. Finally, add the chicken and stir well, then cover and simmer for 30 minutes, or until tender and cooked through. Serve immediately, garnished with extra yogurt.

chicken masala

serves four

⅔ cup plain yogurt
4 tbsp lemon juice
2 tbsp corn oil
2 tsp Garam Masala (see page 7)
2 tsp ground cumin
1 tsp chopped fresh gingerroot
1 tsp chopped garlic
salt
8 skinless, boneless chicken thighs
1 tsp dried fenugreek
2 tsp amchoor (dried mango powder)
1 tsp dried mint
cilantro sprigs, to garnish

TO SERVE
tomato wedges
pappadams

1 Mix the yogurt, lemon juice, corn oil, Garam Masala, cumin, ginger, garlic, and a pinch of salt together in a bowl. Place the chicken thighs in a large, shallow, ovenproof dish. Pour over the yogurt mixture and turn the chicken to coat well. Cover with plastic wrap and let marinate in the refrigerator overnight.

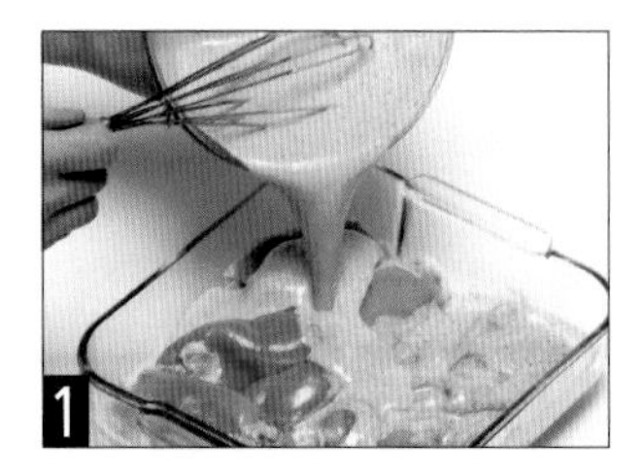
1

2

2 Preheat the oven to 375°F/190°C. Remove the plastic wrap from the chicken and cover the dish with foil. Bake the chicken in its marinade in the preheated oven for 45 minutes. Remove the chicken from the dish with a slotted spoon and cut into bite-size pieces, then spread out on a baking sheet.

3 Stir the fenugreek, amchoor, and mint into the remaining marinade, then pour over the chicken. Return to the oven and bake for an additional 10 minutes. Transfer to a warmed dish, then garnish with cilantro and serve with tomato wedges and pappadams.

3

COOK'S TIP

Fresh garlic adds a wonderful flavor to many dishes, including spicy curries. Store garlic bulbs in a cool, dark place. They will last up to 6 months if kept correctly.

spicy roast chicken

serves four

½ cup ground almonds

½ cup dry unsweetened coconut

⅔ cup vegetable oil

1 onion, finely chopped

1 tsp chopped fresh gingerroot

1 garlic clove, crushed

1 tsp chili powder

1½ tsp Garam Masala (see page 7)

1 tsp salt

⅔ cup plain yogurt

4 chicken quarters, skinned

salad greens, to serve

TO GARNISH

chopped cilantro

1 lemon, cut into wedges

1 Preheat the oven to 325°F/160°C. Dry-roast the almonds and coconut in a heavy-bottom pan, then reserve.

2 Heat the oil in a skillet. Add the onion and cook, stirring, until golden brown.

3 Place the ginger, garlic, chili powder, Garam Masala, and salt in a bowl and mix in the yogurt. Add the reserved almonds and coconut and mix well.

4 Add the onion to the spice mixture and blend, then reserve.

5 Arrange the chicken quarters in the base of a large, heatproof dish. Spoon the spice mixture over the chicken.

6 Cook in the preheated oven for 35–45 minutes. Check that the chicken is cooked thoroughly by piercing the thickest part of the meat with a sharp knife or a fine skewer—the juices will run clear when the chicken is cooked through. Garnish with the cilantro and lemon wedges and serve with a green salad.

COOK'S TIP

For an even spicier dish, add more chili powder and Garam Masala.

chicken dhansak

serves six

generous ½ cup chana dal
generous ½ cup moong dal
generous ½ cup toor dal
generous ½ cup masoor dal
scant ½ cup vegetable oil
2 tsp Garlic Paste (see page 7)
2 tsp Ginger Paste (see page 7)
6 chicken portions
2 cups canned tomatoes, drained
8 oz/225 g peeled pumpkin, diced
3 onions, chopped
4 oz/115 g fresh spinach, chopped
1 eggplant, diced
1 tbsp chopped fresh mint
salt
2 fresh green chilies, chopped
1½ tsp ground turmeric
1 tsp ground coriander
½ tsp ground cardamom
½ tsp ground cinnamon
½ tsp ground cloves
½ tsp chili powder
2 tbsp chopped cilantro, to garnish

1 Place the dals in a large pan and add enough water to cover. Bring to a boil, then reduce the heat and simmer, covered, for 40 minutes. Heat 3 tablespoons of the oil in a skillet. Add half the Garlic Paste and half the Ginger Paste and cook, stirring, for 1 minute. Add the chicken and cook until golden brown. Add to the dals.

2 Stir in the tomatoes, pumpkin, two-thirds of the onion, the spinach, eggplant, mint, and salt to taste. Bring to a boil, then cover and simmer for 45 minutes, or until the chicken is cooked. Transfer the chicken to a plate. Transfer the dal mixture to a food processor and process to a purée.

1

2

3 Heat the remaining oil in a clean pan. Add the remaining onion and cook over low heat for 10 minutes, or until golden. Stir in the chilies and the remaining Garlic Paste and Ginger Paste and cook, stirring, for 2 minutes. Add the remaining spices and cook for 6 minutes, adding a little water if the mixture is very dry. Add to the dal mixture and stir, then cover and simmer for 20 minutes. Add the chicken portions and simmer for an additional 20 minutes. Sprinkle with chopped cilantro and serve.

chicken drumsticks with herbs & spices

serves four

- 8 chicken drumsticks
- 1½ tsp finely chopped fresh gingerroot
- 1–2 garlic cloves, crushed
- 1 tsp salt
- 2 onions, chopped
- ½ large bunch of fresh cilantro, chopped
- 4–6 fresh green chilies, chopped
- 2½ cups vegetable oil
- 4 firm tomatoes, cut into wedges
- 2 large green bell peppers, seeded and coarsely chopped

1 Using a sharp knife, make 2–3 slashes in each chicken drumstick. Rub the ginger, garlic, and salt over the drumsticks and reserve.

2 Place half of the chopped onion, the cilantro, and chilies in a mortar and grind to a paste using a pestle. Rub the paste over the chicken drumsticks.

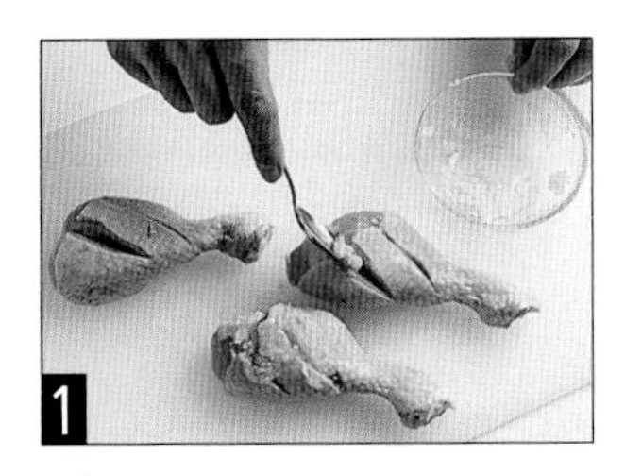

3 Heat the oil in a karahi or large, heavy-bottom skillet. Add the remaining chopped onion and cook until golden brown. Remove the onions from the skillet with a slotted spoon and reserve.

4 Reduce the heat to medium–hot and cook the drumsticks, in batches if necessary, until cooked through (10 minutes per batch).

5 When all of the chicken pieces are cooked, remove them from the skillet and keep warm.

6 Add the tomatoes and bell peppers to the skillet and cook them until they are tender but still firm.

7 Transfer the tomatoes and bell peppers to a serving plate and arrange the drumsticks on top. Garnish with the reserved fried onions.

chicken tossed in black pepper

serves four–six

8 chicken thighs
1 tsp finely chopped fresh gingerroot
1 garlic clove, crushed
1 tsp salt
1½ tsp coarsely ground pepper
⅔ cup vegetable oil
1 green bell pepper, seeded and coarsely sliced
⅔ cup water
2 tbsp lemon juice

FRIED CORN & PEAS
¼ cup unsalted butter
2 cups frozen corn
2 cups frozen peas
½ tsp salt
½ tsp chili powder
1 tbsp lemon juice
chopped cilantro, to garnish

1 Using a sharp knife, bone the chicken thighs, if you prefer.

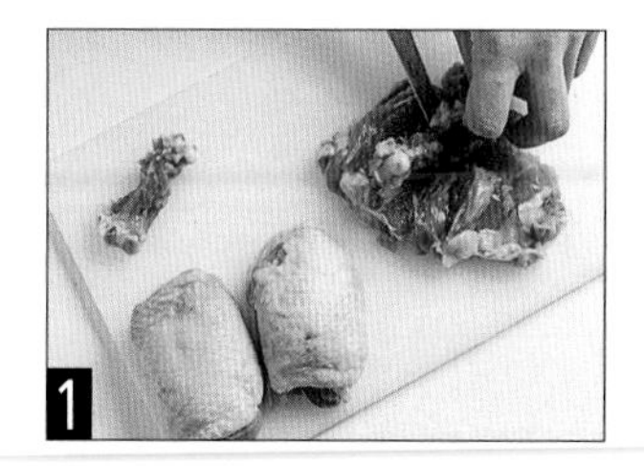
1

2 Mix the ginger, garlic, salt, and pepper together in a small bowl.

2

3 Add the chicken pieces to the pepper mixture and reserve.

4 Heat the oil in a large skillet. Add the chicken pieces and stir-fry for 10 minutes.

5 Reduce the heat and add the green bell pepper and the water to the pan. Let the chicken mixture simmer for 10 minutes, then sprinkle over the lemon juice.

6

6 Meanwhile, make the fried corn and peas. Melt the butter in a separate large skillet. Add the corn and peas and cook, stirring occasionally, for 10 minutes. Add the salt and chili powder and cook for an additional 5 minutes.

7 Sprinkle the lemon juice over the corn and peas and garnish with cilantro.

8 Transfer the chicken and pepper mixture to warmed serving plates and serve immediately with the fried corn and peas.

chicken jalfrezi

serves four

1 tsp mustard oil
3 tbsp vegetable oil
1 large onion, finely chopped
3 garlic cloves, crushed
1 tbsp tomato paste
2 tomatoes, peeled and chopped
1 tsp ground turmeric
½ tsp cumin seeds, ground
½ tsp coriander seeds, ground
½ tsp chili powder
½ tsp Garam Masala (see page 7)
1 tsp red wine vinegar
1 small red bell pepper, seeded and chopped
1 cup frozen fava beans
1 lb/450 g cooked chicken breasts, cut into bite-size pieces
salt
cilantro sprigs, to garnish
freshly cooked rice, to serve

1 Heat the mustard oil in a large skillet set over high heat for 1 minute, until it begins to smoke. Add the vegetable oil and reduce the heat, then add the onion and garlic and cook until they are golden.

2 Add the tomato paste, chopped tomatoes, ground turmeric, cumin, coriander, chili powder, Garam Masala, and red wine vinegar to the pan. Stir the mixture until fragrant.

3 Add the red bell pepper and fava beans and stir for 2 minutes, or until the pepper is softened. Stir in the chicken and salt to taste. Let simmer gently for 6–8 minutes, or until the chicken is heated through and the beans are tender.

4 Transfer to warmed serving plates, then garnish with cilantro sprigs and serve with rice.

COOK'S TIP

This dish is an ideal way of making use of leftover cooked poultry or game birds—turkey, duck, or quail. Any variety of bean works well, or substitute root vegetables, zucchini, potatoes, or broccoli. Leafy vegetables will not be so successful.

chicken & onions

serves four

1¼ cups vegetable oil
4 onions, finely chopped
1½ tsp finely chopped fresh gingerroot
1½ tsp Garam Masala (see page 7)
1 garlic clove, crushed
1 tsp chili powder
1 tsp ground coriander
3 green cardamoms
3 black peppercorns
3 tbsp tomato paste
8 chicken thighs, skinned
1¼ cups water
2 tbsp lemon juice
1 fresh green chili, finely chopped
¼ bunch of cilantro leaves, chopped
1 fresh green chili, cut into strips, to garnish

1 Heat the oil in a large skillet. Add the onions and cook, stirring occasionally, until golden brown.

2 Reduce the heat and add the ginger, Garam Masala, garlic, chili powder, ground coriander, cardamoms, and peppercorns. Stir well.

3 Add the tomato paste to the mixture in the skillet and stir-fry for 5–7 minutes.

4 Add the chicken thighs and toss to coat with the spice mixture.

5 Pour the water into the pan, then cover and let simmer for 20–25 minutes.

6 Add the lemon juice, green chili, and cilantro to the mixture and stir well until mixed.

7 Transfer the chicken and onions to serving plates and garnish with strips of green chili. Serve hot.

chicken korma

serves eight

1½ tsp finely chopped fresh gingerroot
1–2 garlic cloves, crushed
2 tsp Garam Masala (see page 7)
1 tsp chili powder
1 tsp salt
1 tsp black cumin seeds
3 green cardamoms, with husks removed and seeds crushed
1 tsp ground coriander
1 tsp ground almonds
⅔ cup plain yogurt
8 skinless, boneless chicken breasts
1¼ cups vegetable oil
2 onions, sliced
⅔ cup water
¼ bunch of cilantro, chopped
2 fresh green chilies, chopped
freshly cooked rice, to serve

1 Mix the ginger, garlic, Garam Masala, chili powder, salt, cumin seeds, cardamoms, ground coriander, almonds, and yogurt together in a small bowl.

2 Place the chicken breasts in a dish and spoon over the yogurt and spice mixture. Let chill.

3 Heat the oil in a large skillet. Add the onions and cook until golden brown.

4 Add the chicken breasts to the skillet and stir-fry for 5–7 minutes.

5 Add the water, then cover and let simmer for 20–25 minutes.

6 Add the cilantro and chilies and cook for an additional 10 minutes, gently stirring occasionally.

7 Transfer to a serving plate and serve with freshly cooked rice.

1

2

4

tandoori-style chicken

serves four

8 chicken drumsticks, skinned
⅔ cup plain yogurt
1½ tsp finely chopped fresh gingerroot
1–2 garlic cloves, crushed
1 tsp chili powder
2 tsp ground cumin
2 tsp ground coriander
1 tsp salt
½ tsp red food coloring (optional)
1 tbsp tamarind paste
⅔ cup water
⅔ cup vegetable oil, for basting
lettuce leaves
Naan Bread (see page 177), to serve

TO GARNISH
onion rings
1 lemon, cut into wedges

1 Using a sharp knife, make 2–3 slashes in each chicken drumstick. Place the yogurt in a large bowl. Add the ginger, garlic, chili powder, ground cumin, ground coriander, salt, and red food coloring (if using) and blend together.

2 Add the chicken to the yogurt and spice mixture and mix to coat well. Let the chicken marinate in the refrigerator for a minimum of 3 hours.

3 Mix the tamarind paste and water together in a separate bowl, then fold into the yogurt and spice mixture. Toss the drumsticks in this mixture and let marinate in the refrigerator for an additional 3 hours.

COOK'S TIP

Before serving the chicken drumsticks, make sure the chicken is tender and thoroughly cooked. A Raita, such as Mint Raita (see page 222), complements this dish perfectly.

4 Preheat the broiler to medium. Transfer the drumsticks to a heatproof dish and brush the drumsticks with a little oil. Cook under the hot broiler for 30–35 minutes, turning the drumsticks occasionally and basting.

5 Arrange the chicken on a bed of lettuce and garnish with onion rings and lemon wedges. Serve with Naan Bread.

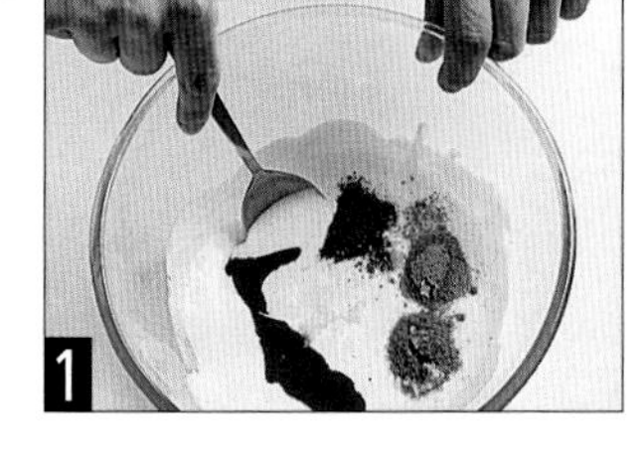
1

2

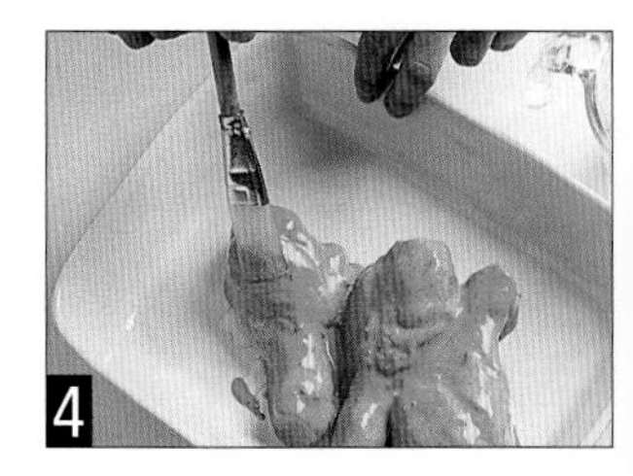
4

chicken dopiaza

serves four

- 3 tbsp ghee or vegetable oil
- 8 baby onions or shallots, halved
- 3 dried red chilies
- 6 cardamoms
- 6 black peppercorns
- 2 whole cloves
- 2 bay leaves
- 2 onions, finely chopped
- 1 tsp Garlic Paste (see page 7)
- 1 tsp Ginger Paste (see page 7)
- 1 tsp ground cumin
- 1 tsp ground coriander
- 1 tsp chili powder
- ½ tsp ground turmeric
- 1 cup canned tomatoes
- 4 tbsp water
- 8 skinless chicken thighs
- cilantro leaves, to garnish
- freshly cooked rice, to serve

1 Heat 2 tablespoons of the ghee in a large, heavy-bottom pan or flameproof casserole. Add the baby onions and cook over low heat, stirring occasionally, for 10 minutes, or until golden. Remove with a slotted spoon and reserve until required.

2 Add the remaining ghee to the pan and cook the chilies, cardamoms, peppercorns, cloves, and bay leaves, stirring constantly, for 2 minutes, or until they give off their aroma. Add the chopped onions and cook, stirring frequently, for 5 minutes, or until softened.

3 Stir in the Garlic Paste, Ginger Paste, cumin, ground coriander, chili powder, and turmeric and cook, stirring constantly, for 2 minutes. Add the tomatoes and their can juices and the water. Stir well and simmer for 5 minutes, or until slightly thickened.

4 Add the chicken thighs and simmer for 20 minutes. Return the baby onions to the pan and cook for an additional 10 minutes, or until the chicken is tender and cooked through. Serve immediately with rice, garnished with cilantro leaves.

VARIATION

You could use 8 skinless chicken drumsticks or 4 larger chicken portions. Increase the cooking time by 15 minutes for chicken portions.

COOK'S TIP

This dish can be prepared a day in advance and cooled, then covered and stored in the refrigerator. It is, however, not suitable for freezing.

chicken patties

serves six–eight

3 lb 5 oz/1.5 kg chicken, boned
½ tsp ground cumin
4 cardamom seeds, crushed
½ tsp ground cinnamon
1 tsp salt
1 tsp finely chopped fresh gingerroot
1 garlic clove, crushed
½ tsp ground allspice
½ tsp pepper
1¼ cups water
2 tbsp plain yogurt
2 fresh green chilies
1 small onion, chopped
½ bunch of cilantro, chopped
1 egg, beaten
1¼ cups vegetable oil
1 lemon, cut into wedges, to garnish

1 Place the chicken in a large pan. Add the ground cumin, cardamom seeds, ground cinnamon, salt, ginger, garlic, allspice, and pepper and pour in the water. Bring the mixture to a boil and boil until all of the water has been absorbed.

2 Place the mixture in a food processor and process to a smooth paste. Transfer the paste to a large bowl. Add the yogurt and blend together until well mixed.

3 Place the chilies, onion, and cilantro in the food processor and process until finely ground. Add to the chicken mixture and combine. Add the beaten egg and mix well.

4 With dampened hands, divide the mixture into 12 portions and shape into small flat circles.

5 Heat the oil in a pan. Add the rounds in batches and cook gently, turning once. Drain thoroughly on paper towels and serve hot, garnished with lemon wedges.

COOK'S TIP

You can serve these patties with any dal, such as Onion Dal (see page 158), a green salad, and Chapatis (see page 185).

buttered chicken

serves four–six

scant ⅔ cup unsalted butter
1 tbsp vegetable oil
2 onions, finely chopped
1 tsp finely chopped or crushed fresh gingerroot
2 tsp Garam Masala (see page 7)
2 tsp ground coriander
1 tsp chili powder
1 tsp black cumin seeds
1 garlic clove, crushed
1 tsp salt
3 green cardamoms
3 black peppercorns
⅔ cup plain yogurt
2 tbsp tomato paste
8 chicken pieces, skinned
⅔ cup water
2 bay leaves
⅔ cup light cream
TO GARNISH
chopped cilantro
2 fresh green chilies, chopped

1 Heat the butter and oil in a large skillet. Add the onions and cook until golden brown, stirring. Reduce the heat.

2 Place the ginger in a bowl. Add the Garam Masala, ground coriander, chili powder, cumin seeds, garlic, salt, cardamoms, and peppercorns and blend. Add the yogurt and tomato paste and stir well.

3 Add the chicken pieces to the yogurt and spice mixture and mix to coat well.

4 Add the chicken to the onions in the skillet and stir-fry vigorously, making semicircular movements, for 5–7 minutes.

5 Add the water and bay leaves and let simmer for 30 minutes, stirring occasionally.

6 Add the cream and cook for an additional 10–15 minutes. Garnish with cilantro and chilies and serve.

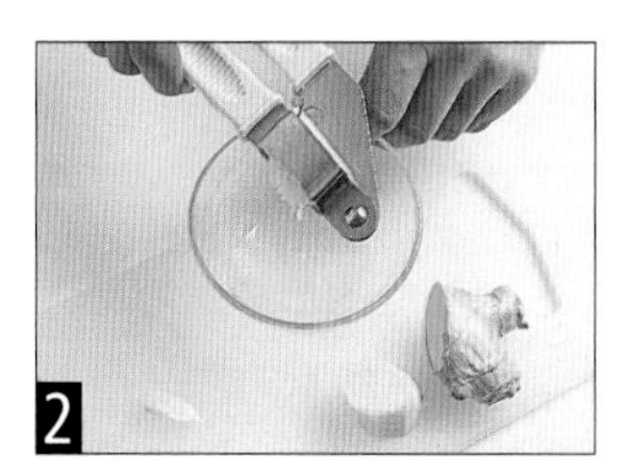

duck curry

serves four

2-inch/5-cm piece fresh gingerroot
3 onions
2½ cups chicken stock
3 garlic cloves, finely chopped
4 whole cloves
salt
4 tbsp ghee or vegetable oil
1 tsp cayenne pepper
2 tsp coriander seeds, lightly crushed
6 lb/2.7 kg duck, cut into portions
large pinch of saffron threads
generous 1 cup ground almonds
1¼ cups single cream
1 tsp cardamom seeds, lightly crushed

1 Preheat the oven to 300°F/150°C. Finely chop the ginger and reserve. Cut 1 onion in half and finely chop the others. Place the stock in a large, heavy-bottom pan, then add the onion halves, ginger, garlic, cloves, and a pinch of salt and bring to a boil. Boil until reduced by half, then strain into a bowl and reserve until required. Discard the contents of the strainer.

2 Heat the ghee in a flameproof casserole. Add the chopped onions and cook over low heat for 10 minutes, or until golden. Stir in the cayenne and coriander seeds and cook for 1 minute, or until they give off their aroma. Add the duck portions and cook, turning frequently, until browned all over. Add the reserved stock, then season with salt to taste and bring to a boil. Reduce the heat, then cover and cook for 20 minutes.

3 Place the saffron in a bowl and add enough boiling water to cover. Let soak for 10 minutes. Mix the almonds, cream, cardamom seeds, and the saffron with its soaking liquid together. Pour the mixture into the casserole and stir well. Transfer to the preheated oven and cook for an additional 20 minutes, or until the duck is tender. Serve immediately.

COOK'S TIP

It is best to use homemade stock for this dish, if possible. If you have to use a stock cube, don't add any salt in Step 1, because stock cubes tend to be very salty.

southern duck

serves four

- 2 tsp cumin seeds
- 2 tsp coriander seeds
- 1 tsp cardamom seeds
- 2 tsp Garam Masala (see page 7)
- 1 tsp chili powder
- ½ tsp ground turmeric
- salt
- 6 boneless duck breasts
- 2 garlic cloves, finely chopped
- 2 onions, sliced
- 3¾ cups canned coconut milk
- ½ cup white wine vinegar
- ¾ cup water
- 2 tbsp chopped cilantro

COOK'S TIP

Using a sharp knife, trim off any excess fat from the duck breasts before cooking them, but do not remove the skin.

1 Place the cumin, coriander, and cardamom seeds, Garam Masala, chili powder, and turmeric into a mortar or spice grinder with a pinch of salt and grind finely. Reserve.

2 Place the duck breasts, skin-side down, in a large, heavy-bottom skillet and cook over medium heat for 10 minutes, or until the skin is golden brown. Turn over and cook for an additional 6–8 minutes, or until the second side is browned. Remove from the skillet with a slotted spoon and drain on paper towels.

2

3 Drain off all but about 1 tablespoon of the fat from the skillet and return to the heat. Add the garlic and onions and cook, stirring occasionally, for 8 minutes, or until golden brown. Stir in the ground spice mixture and cook, stirring constantly, for 2 minutes, or until the spices give off their aroma.

3

4 Return the duck breasts to the skillet and stir in the coconut milk, vinegar, and water. Bring to a boil, then reduce the heat and simmer, covered, for 40–45 minutes, or until the duck is tender. Taste and add more salt, if necessary. Stir in the chopped cilantro and serve immediately.

4

Fish Dishes

Fish is one of the most versatile ingredients and is equally delicious in spicy curries and creamy stews or when presented as fragrantly marinated kabobs. In this chapter, there are delicious recipes for both freshwater and sea fish, as well as many great ways of cooking shrimp.

Fish is eaten in the south and west of India, and traditional recipes are included, such as the delicious south Indian Fish in Coconut Sauce (see page 98) and Baked Fish with Coconut & Cilantro (see page 100), a classic Parsee dish from the west coast. The fish is traditionally cooked in banana leaves, which are available from specialty Asian food stores, but waxed paper can be used instead.

fried fish in besan

serves four–six

- ⅔ cup besan
- 1 tsp finely chopped fresh gingerroot
- 1 garlic clove, crushed
- 2 tsp chili powder
- 1 tsp salt
- ½ tsp ground turmeric
- 2 fresh green chilies, chopped
- ¼ bunch of cilantro, chopped
- 1¼ cups water
- 2 lb 4 oz/1 kg skinless cod fillet
- 1¼ cups oil
- freshly cooked rice, to serve

TO GARNISH

- 2 lemons, cut into wedges
- 3 fresh green chilies, cut into strips

COOK'S TIP

Besan (gram flour) or chana dal flour (lentil flour) is used to make Pakoras (see page 190) and is also used to bind kabobs. A combination of besan and ordinary whole-wheat flour makes a delicious Gram Flour Bread (see page 182).

1 Place the besan in a large bowl. Add the ginger, garlic, chili powder, salt, and turmeric and mix to blend well.

2 Add the chopped chilies and cilantro to the spiced mixture and stir to mix.

3 Pour in the water and stir to form a thick batter. Reserve.

4 Using a sharp knife, cut the cod into 10–12 pieces.

5 Carefully dip the pieces of cod into the batter, coating the cod all over. Shake off any excess batter.

6 Heat the oil in a heavy-bottom skillet. Add the battered cod and cook, in batches, over medium heat, turning once, until the fish is cooked through and golden.

7 Transfer the battered cod to a serving dish and garnish with the lemon wedges and green chilies. Serve with freshly cooked rice.

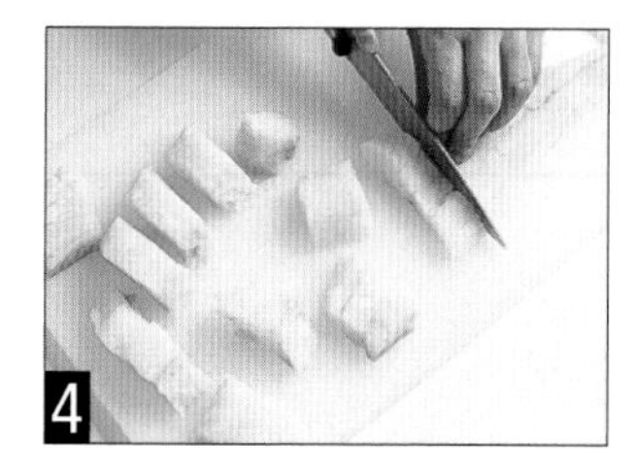

fish in tomato sauce

serves four–six

1 lb 2 oz/500 g tomatoes
4 fresh green chilies
2 lb 4 oz/1 kg haddock fillets, skinned
salt
2 tsp ground turmeric
4 tbsp ghee or vegetable oil
2 onions, sliced
1 tbsp ground coriander
2 tsp Garam Masala (see page 7)
1 tsp chili powder
1 tsp sugar
2 tbsp plain yogurt
1 tbsp lemon juice
cilantro sprigs, to garnish
Pilaf Rice (see page 166), to serve

1 Peel, seed, and chop the tomatoes, then reserve. Using a sharp knife, slit the chilies lengthwise along 1 side, then seed and reserve. Remove any pin bones from the fish and cut into large chunks. Mix 1 teaspoon of salt and 1½ teaspoons of the turmeric together in a bowl, then rub the mixture all over the fish.

2 Heat the ghee in a large skillet. Add the fish, in batches if necessary, and cook over medium heat, stirring frequently, until golden brown all over. Remove with a slotted spoon and reserve. Add the onions, then reduce the heat and cook, stirring occasionally, for 10 minutes, or until golden brown.

2

3

4

3 Stir in the remaining turmeric, the coriander, Garam Masala, chili powder, and sugar and cook, stirring, for an additional 2 minutes. Increase the heat to medium and add the tomatoes, yogurt, lemon juice, and reserved chilies. Bring to a boil, then reduce the heat and simmer for 15 minutes.

4 Return the fish to the skillet. Stir gently to coat well in the sauce. Simmer for an additional 10 minutes, or until the fish is cooked. Taste and adjust the seasoning, then garnish with cilantro and serve with Pilaf Rice.

punjabi-style fish

serves four

2 tbsp ghee or vegetable oil
2 onions, sliced
1 tsp Garlic Paste (see page 7)
1 tsp Ginger Paste (see page 7)
1 tbsp ground cumin
2 tsp ground coriander
1 tsp Garam Masala (see page 7)
½ tsp ground cinnamon
½ tsp cayenne pepper
4 cardamoms, lightly crushed
salt
4 cups canned tomatoes
½ cup light cream
1 tbsp lemon juice
1 lb 12 oz/800 g cod fillets, skinned and cut into 1½-inch/4-cm slices
chopped cilantro, to garnish
freshly cooked rice, to serve

1 Heat the ghee in a pan. Add the onions and cook over low heat, stirring occasionally, for 10 minutes, or until golden. Add the Garlic Paste, Ginger Paste, cumin, ground coriander, Garam Masala, cinnamon, cayenne, cardamoms, and a pinch of salt and cook, stirring, for 2 minutes, or until the spices give off their aroma.

2 Stir in the tomatoes and their can juices, cream, and lemon juice and cook, stirring occasionally, for 5 minutes, or until slightly thickened. Do not let the mixture boil.

3 Add the pieces of fish, then cover and simmer gently for 10 minutes, or until tender. Transfer to warmed serving dishes and sprinkle with chopped cilantro. Serve with rice.

COOK'S TIP

It is important not to let the sauce boil in Step 2 because light cream has a tendency to curdle when heated, especially in the presence of an acidic ingredient such as lemon juice.

VARIATION

Any firm-fleshed white fish fillet, such as angler fish or haddock, would work well in this dish.

fried trout with ginger

serves four

1 tsp Ginger Paste (see page 7)
1 tsp Garlic Paste (see page 7)
2 fresh green chilies, seeded and finely chopped
1 tbsp chopped cilantro
¼ tsp ground turmeric
salt and pepper
4 trout, cleaned
vegetable oil, for brushing
TO GARNISH
cilantro sprigs
lime slices

1 Preheat the broiler to medium. Mix the Ginger Paste, Garlic Paste, chilies, cilantro, turmeric, 1 teaspoon of pepper, and a pinch of salt together in a small bowl. Stir in enough water to make a smooth paste.

2 Using a sharp knife, slash the trout diagonally on both sides 2–3 times. Rub the spice paste into the fish, especially the slashes.

3 Brush with oil and cook under the hot broiler for 15 minutes, turning once and brushing with more oil. Transfer to warmed serving plates and garnish with cilantro sprigs and lime slices. Serve immediately.

COOK'S TIP

Cilantro is used extensively in Indian cooking and imparts a distinctive flavor to dishes. Finely chop the stems as well as the leaves of the herb.

bengali-style fish

serves four–six

1 tsp ground turmeric
1 tsp salt
2 lb 4 oz/1 kg cod fillet, skinned and cut into pieces
6 tbsp corn oil
4 fresh green chilies
1 tsp finely chopped fresh gingerroot
1 garlic clove, crushed
2 onions, finely chopped
2 tomatoes, finely chopped
6 tbsp mustard oil
1¾ cups water
chopped cilantro, to garnish
Naan Bread (see page 177), to serve

COOK'S TIP

In the hot and humid eastern plains that surround Bengal, the mustard plant flourishes, providing oil for cooking and spicy seeds for flavoring. Fish and seafood feature in many meals, often flavored with mustard oil.

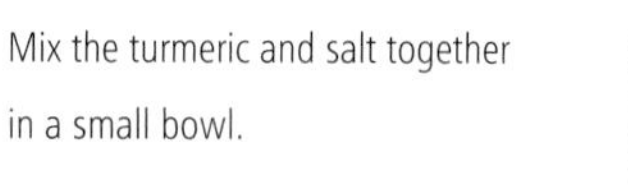

1 Mix the turmeric and salt together in a small bowl.

2 Spoon the turmeric and salt mixture over the fish pieces.

3 Heat the corn oil in a skillet. Add the fish and cook until pale yellow. Remove the fish with a slotted spoon and reserve.

4 Place the chilies, ginger, garlic, onions, tomatoes, and mustard oil in a mortar and, using a pestle, grind to form a paste. Alternatively, process the ingredients in a food processor.

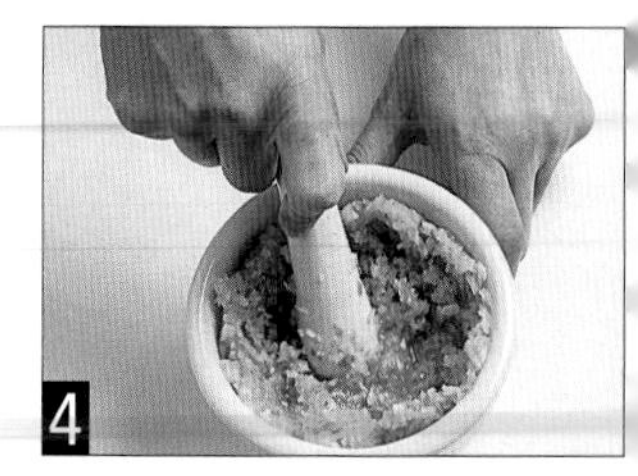

5 Transfer the spice paste to a skillet and dry-fry until golden brown.

6 Remove the skillet from the heat and gently place the fish pieces into the paste without breaking the fish up.

7 Return the skillet to the heat, then add the water and cook the fish, uncovered, over medium heat for 15–20 minutes.

7

8 Garnish with chopped cilantro and serve with Naan Bread.

deep-fried fish

serves six

8 red snapper fillets, halved
salt and pepper
½ cup lemon juice
vegetable oil, for deep-frying
2 limes, cut into wedges, to garnish

BATTER
generous ½ cup besan
2 tbsp rice flour
1 tsp chili powder
1 tsp ground turmeric
½ cup water

1 Season the fish to taste with salt and pepper, then place in a large, shallow, nonmetallic dish and sprinkle with the lemon juice. Cover with plastic wrap and let marinate in a cool place for 30 minutes.

2 Meanwhile, make the batter. Sift together the besan, rice flour, chili powder, and turmeric into a large bowl. Gradually stir in the water to make a smooth batter. Cover and let rest for 30 minutes.

3 Heat the oil for deep-frying in a deep-fat fryer or large, heavy-bottom pan to 350–375°F/180–190°C, or until a cube of bread browns in 30 seconds. Dip the fish pieces in the batter a few at a time, to coat, and drain off the excess. Add to the hot oil and deep-fry for 5 minutes, or until golden brown and crisp. Remove with a slotted spoon and drain on paper towels. Keep warm while you cook the remaining pieces of fish. Serve, garnished with lime wedges.

COOK'S TIP

Make sure that the batter is well blended before resting. If you let the batter rest for more than 30 minutes, stir it well before using, because it may have begun to separate.

angler fish kabobs

serves four

3 tbsp lime juice
1 tbsp finely chopped fresh mint
1 tbsp finely chopped cilantro
2 fresh green chilies, seeded and finely chopped
1 tsp Ginger Paste (see page 7)
½ tsp Garlic Paste (see page 7)
1 tsp ground coriander
salt
12 oz /350 g angler fish fillet, cubed
1 red bell pepper, seeded and cut into chunks
1 green bell pepper, seeded and cut into chunks
8 baby corn cobs, halved
8 white mushrooms
8 cherry tomatoes
½ small cauliflower, broken into florets
1 tbsp corn oil
Pilaf Rice (see page 166), to serve
TO GARNISH
1 lime, cut into wedges
cilantro sprigs

1 Mix the lime juice, mint, cilantro, chilies, Ginger Paste, Garlic Paste, ground coriander, and a pinch of salt together in a large, shallow, nonmetallic dish. Add the fish and stir to coat. Cover with plastic wrap and let marinate in a cool place for 30 minutes.

2 Preheat the broiler to medium. Drain the fish and reserve the marinade. Thread the angler fish, chunks of bell pepper, baby corn cobs, mushrooms, cherry tomatoes, and cauliflower florets onto 4 long or 8 short skewers.

3 Brush the kabobs with any remaining marinade and the oil and cook under the hot broiler, turning and basting frequently, for 10 minutes, or until cooked. Serve immediately on a bed of Pilaf Rice, garnished with lime wedges and cilantro sprigs.

COOK'S TIP

If using wooden or bamboo skewers, remember to soak them in a bowl of warm water while the fish is marinating to prevent them charring under the broiler.

VARIATION

Substitute large raw shrimp, peeled but with their tails left intact, for the angler fish, if you like.

fish in coconut sauce

serves six

1 tbsp ghee or vegetable oil
2 onions, sliced
2 tsp ground cumin
1 tsp Garlic Paste (see page 7)
1 tsp ground coriander
1 tsp ground turmeric
4 whole cloves
4 cardamoms, lightly crushed
6 curry leaves
3 cups canned coconut milk
2 lb 4 oz/1 kg angler fish tail
Chapatis (see page 185), to serve

COOK'S TIP

Try to make sure that all the pieces of fish are about the same size and thickness, so that they cook evenly. To test if the fish is cooked through, the flesh should be opaque and flake easily.

1 Heat the ghee in a large, heavy-bottom pan. Add the onions and cook over low heat, stirring occasionally, for 10 minutes, or until golden. Stir in the cumin, Garlic Paste, ground coriander, turmeric, cloves, and cardamoms and cook, stirring constantly, for 1–2 minutes, or until the spices give off their aroma. Add the curry leaves and coconut milk, then stir well and simmer for 20 minutes.

2 Meanwhile, remove and discard any gray membrane from the angler fish. Using a sharp knife, cut down either side of the central bone and remove and discard it. Cut each fillet in half across the center, then slice in half horizontally. Roll up each piece of fish as tightly as possible.

3 Gently add the fish rolls to the coconut sauce. Cover, then simmer for an additional 10 minutes, or until the fish is tender and cooked through. Use the curry leaves as a garnish and serve immediately with Chapatis.

1

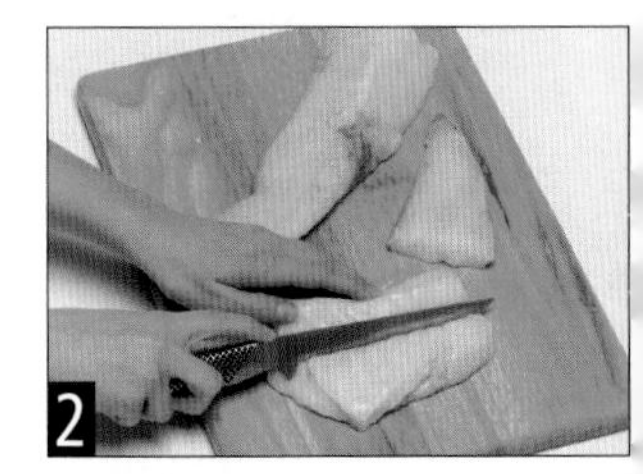
2

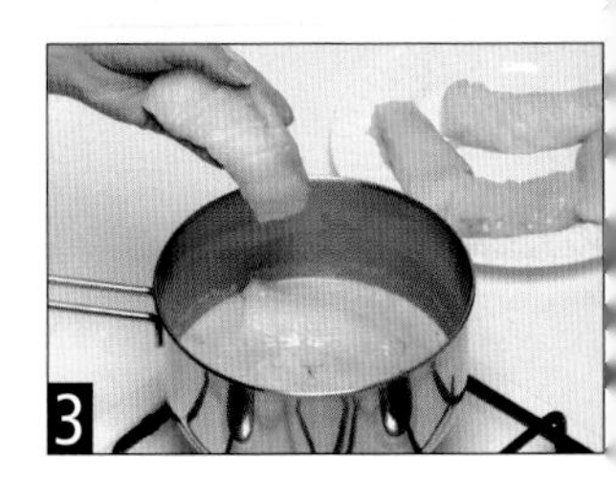
3

baked fish with coconut & cilantro

serves four

2 large lemon sole, cleaned and scaled
salt
5 tbsp lemon juice
scant 2 cups cilantro, chopped
½ cup dry unsweetened coconut
6 fresh green chilies, seeded and chopped
4 garlic cloves, chopped
1 tsp cumin seeds
1 tbsp sugar
vegetable oil, for brushing

1 Using a sharp knife, slash the fish diagonally twice on both sides. Rub all over the inside and outside of the fish with salt and 4 tablespoons of the lemon juice. Place on a large plate, then cover and let marinate in a cool place for 30 minutes.

COOK'S TIP

Do not marinate the fish in the lemon juice for longer than an hour, otherwise the acid begins to denature the protein and "cook" the fish.

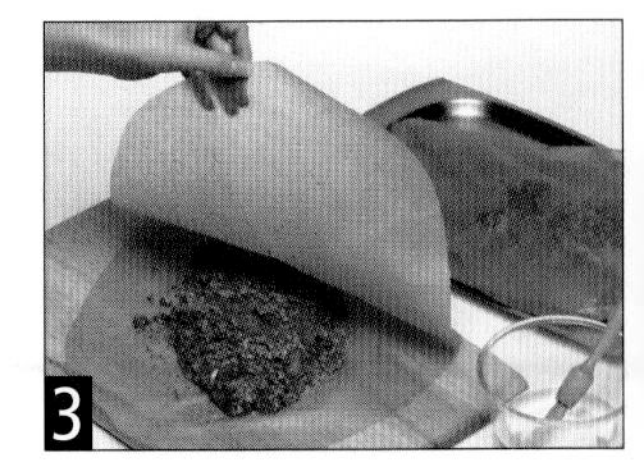

2 Preheat the oven to 400°F/200°C. Place the remaining lemon juice, cilantro, coconut, chilies, garlic, cumin seeds, and sugar in a food processor and process until smooth. Alternatively, place the ingredients in a mortar and grind with a pestle.

3 Cut out 2 pieces of parchment paper or waxed paper large enough to enclose a fish completely, and brush with a little oil. Rub the fish all over with the coconut and cilantro paste, then place each fish on a piece of parchment paper or waxed paper and fold in the sides to enclose. Place the packages on a large baking sheet and bake in the preheated oven for 25–30 minutes, or until cooked through. Unwrap and serve immediately.

marinated fish

serves four

1 fresh green chili
4 red snapper, cleaned
½ cup lime juice
4 tbsp plain yogurt
1 tsp Garlic Paste (see page 7)
1 tsp Ginger Paste (see page 7)
1 tbsp coriander seeds
1 tsp Garam Masala (see page 7)
few drops red food coloring (optional)
¾ stick butter
2 tsp ground cumin

TO GARNISH
1 lime, cut into wedges
cilantro sprigs

1 Seed and chop the chili and reserve. Using a sharp knife, slash the fish diagonally several times on both sides and sprinkle with the lime juice. Place the yogurt, Garlic Paste, Ginger Paste, coriander seeds, chopped chili, and Garam Masala in a food processor and process to make a paste. Transfer to a large, shallow dish and stir in the red food coloring (if using). Add the fish, turning to coat. Cover with plastic wrap and let marinate in the refrigerator for 8 hours, turning occasionally.

1

COOK'S TIP

Do not let the butter turn brown when you are melting it over low heat, otherwise it will taste bitter and may spoil the finished dish.

2 Preheat the oven to 375°F/190°C. Remove the fish from the marinade and place on a wire rack in a large roasting pan. Cook in the preheated oven for 10 minutes.

2

3 Meanwhile, melt the butter in a small pan over low heat. Remove the pan from the heat and stir in the cumin. Brush the butter all over the fish and return to the oven for an additional 6–7 minutes, or until cooked through. Transfer to warmed plates and garnish with lime wedges and cilantro sprigs. Serve immediately.

3

shrimp with tomatoes

serves four–six

3 onions
1 green bell pepper
1 tsp finely chopped fresh gingerroot
1 garlic clove, crushed
1 tsp salt
1 tsp chili powder
2 tbsp lemon juice
12 oz /350 g frozen shrimp
3 tbsp vegetable oil
2 cups canned tomatoes
chopped cilantro, to garnish
freshly cooked rice, to serve

COOK'S TIP

Fresh gingerroot looks rather like a knobbly potato. The skin should be peeled, then the flesh either grated, finely chopped, or sliced. Ginger is also available ground: this can be used as a substitute for fresh gingerroot, but the flavor of the fresh root is far superior.

1 Using a sharp knife, slice the onions and seed and slice the green bell pepper.

2 Place the ginger, garlic, salt, and chili powder in a small bowl and mix well. Add the lemon juice and mix to make a paste.

3 Place the shrimp in a bowl of cold water and let thaw. Drain thoroughly.

4 Heat the oil in a medium-size skillet. Add the onions and cook until golden brown.

5 Add the spice paste to the onions. Reduce the heat to low and cook, stirring and mixing well, for 3 minutes.

6 Add the canned tomatoes with their juice and the sliced bell pepper, and cook for 5–7 minutes, stirring occasionally.

7 Add the thawed shrimp to the pan and cook for 10 minutes, stirring occasionally. Garnish with cilantro and serve hot with freshly cooked rice.

shrimp with bell peppers

serves four

1 lb/450 g frozen shrimp

½ bunch of cilantro

1 garlic clove, crushed

1 tsp salt

1 red bell pepper

1 green bell pepper

scant 5 tbsp unsalted butter

cilantro sprigs, to garnish

freshly cooked rice, to serve

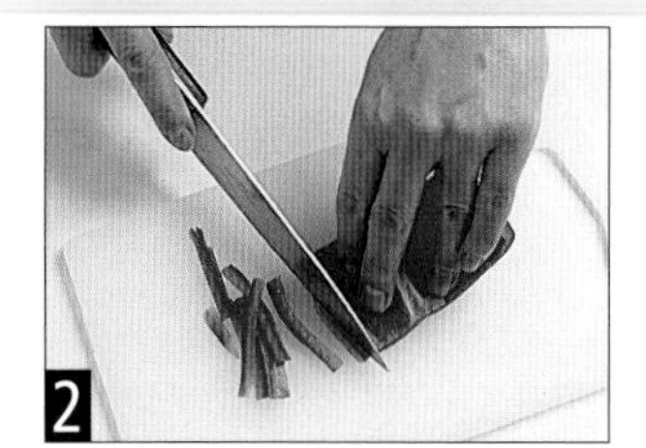

1 Thaw the shrimp and rinse under cold running water twice. Drain the shrimp thoroughly and place in a large bowl.

2 Finely chop the cilantro and add to the shrimp with the garlic and salt. Reserve until required. Seed and slice the red and green bell peppers and reserve until required.

3 Melt the butter in a large skillet. Add the shrimp and stir-fry, stirring and tossing the shrimp gently, for 10–12 minutes.

4 Add the reserved bell peppers and cook for an additional 3–5 minutes, stirring occasionally.

5 Transfer the shrimp and bell peppers to a serving dish. Garnish with cilantro sprigs and serve with rice.

COOK'S TIP

When using frozen shrimp, make sure that they are thoroughly thawed before using. Store them, covered, in the refrigerator until needed and always use the same day as thawed.

tandoori-style shrimp

serves four

10–12 raw jumbo shrimp
scant ½ cup unsalted butter
1 tsp finely chopped fresh gingerroot
1 garlic clove, crushed
1 tsp chili powder
½ tsp salt
1 tsp ground coriander
1 tsp ground cumin
½ bunch of cilantro, finely chopped
few drops of red food coloring (optional)
8 lettuce leaves
TO GARNISH
1–2 fresh green chilies, finely chopped
1 lemon, cut into wedges

COOK'S TIP

Though not essential, it is best to shell the shrimp before cooking them, because some people find it slightly awkward to peel them at the table.

1 Preheat the broiler to high. Carefully shell the shrimp.

2 Transfer the shelled shrimp to a flameproof dish.

3 Melt the butter in a pan, then remove from the heat.

4 Add the ginger, garlic, chili powder, salt, ground coriander, ground cumin, chopped cilantro, and the red food coloring (if using) to the butter and mix together well.

5 Brush the melted butter and spice mixture over the shrimp.

6 Cook the shrimp under the broiler, for 10 minutes, turning once.

7 Arrange the shrimp on a bed of lettuce and garnish with finely chopped chilies and lemon wedges. Serve immediately.

dried shrimp

serves four

7 oz/200 g dried shrimp
1¼ cups vegetable oil
2 onions, sliced
3 fresh green chilies, finely chopped
¼ bunch of cilantro, finely chopped
1½ tsp finely chopped fresh gingerroot
1–2 garlic cloves, crushed
pinch of ground turmeric
1 tsp salt
1 tsp chili powder, plus extra to garnish
2 tbsp lemon juice
Chapatis (see page 185), to serve

1 Soak the shrimp in a bowl of cold water for 2 hours. Drain the shrimp thoroughly and rinse under cold running water twice. Drain the shrimp again, thoroughly.

2 Heat ⅔ cup of the oil in a large skillet.

3 Add the onions, chilies, and the chopped cilantro to the skillet and stir-fry until the onions are golden brown.

VARIATION

You could use 1 lb/450 g fresh shrimp instead of the dried shrimp, if you prefer.

4 Add the ginger, garlic, turmeric, salt, and chili powder to the pan and stir-fry for an additional 2 minutes over low heat. Reserve until required.

5 Heat the remaining oil in a pan. Add the shrimp and cook, stirring occasionally, until the shrimp are crisp.

6 Add the shrimp to the onions and blend together. Return the shrimp and onion mixture to the heat and stir-fry for an additional 3–5 minutes. Sprinkle over the lemon juice.

7 Transfer the shrimp to a serving dish. Garnish with a pinch of chili powder and serve with Chapatis.

shrimp with spinach

serves four–six

- 8 oz/225 g frozen shrimp
- 12 oz /350 g canned spinach purée or frozen spinach, thawed and chopped
- 2 tomatoes
- ⅔ cup vegetable oil
- ½ tsp mustard seeds
- ½ tsp onion seeds
- 1 tsp finely chopped fresh gingerroot
- 1 garlic clove, crushed
- 1 tsp chili powder
- 1 tsp salt

1. Place the shrimp in a bowl of cold water and let stand until thawed thoroughly.

2. Drain the can of spinach purée (if using).

3. Using a sharp knife, cut the tomatoes into slices.

4. Heat the oil in a large skillet. Add the mustard and onion seeds to the skillet.

5. Reduce the heat and add the tomatoes, spinach, ginger, garlic, chili powder, and salt to the skillet and stir-fry for 5–7 minutes.

6. Drain the shrimp thoroughly and add to the spinach mixture in the skillet.

7. Gently stir the shrimp and spinach mixture until well blended, then cover and let simmer over low heat for 7–10 minutes.

8. Transfer the shrimp and spinach to a serving dish and serve hot.

COOK'S TIP

If using frozen spinach, it should be thawed and squeezed dry before using. You could use fresh spinach, if you prefer.

4

5

5

mussels in coconut sauce

serves four

3 tbsp ghee or vegetable oil
1 onion, finely chopped
1 tsp Garlic Paste (see page 7)
1 tsp Ginger Paste (see page 7)
1 tsp ground cumin
1 tsp ground coriander
½ tsp ground turmeric
salt
2½ cups canned coconut milk
2 lb 4 oz/1 kg live mussels, scrubbed and debearded
chopped cilantro, to garnish

COOK'S TIP

To prepare mussels, scrub them well under cold running water and pull off any beards that are still attached to them. Discard any with broken shells or that do not shut when sharply tapped.

1 Heat the ghee in a large, heavy-bottom skillet. Add the onion and cook over low heat, stirring occasionally, for 10 minutes, or until golden brown.

2 Add the Garlic Paste and Ginger Paste and cook, stirring constantly, for 2 minutes. Add the cumin, ground coriander, turmeric, and a pinch of salt and cook, stirring constantly, for an additional 2 minutes. Stir in the coconut milk and bring the mixture to a boil.

3 Add the mussels, then cover and cook for 5 minutes, or until the mussels have opened. Discard any mussels that remain shut. Transfer the mussels, with the coconut sauce, to a large, warmed serving dish. Sprinkle with cilantro and serve immediately.

VARIATION

Substitute 2 cooked crabs for the mussels. Add the crab meat with the claws in Step 3 and cook until just heated through.

Vegetables

A great many people in India are vegetarians, and over the years Indians have used their imagination to create a vast number of different vegetarian dishes. Spinach, tomatoes, potatoes, green beans, and cauliflower are all commonly used in Indian cooking. Other popular ingredients, including eggplants, okra, and daikon, are less familiar in the Western culinary repertoire, despite the fact that they are now widely available. This chapter includes some simple but delicious vegetarian dishes. Serve them as an accompaniment to other curries, or as vegetarian dishes in their own right.

green bean & potato curry

serves four

1¼ cups vegetable oil
1 tsp white cumin seeds
1 tsp mixed mustard and onion seeds
4 dried red chilies
3 tomatoes, sliced
1 tsp salt
1 tsp finely chopped fresh gingerroot
1 garlic clove, crushed
1 tsp chili powder
1⅓ cups green beans, sliced
2 potatoes, peeled and diced
1¼ cups water
chopped cilantro
2 fresh green chilies, finely chopped

COOK'S TIP

Mustard seeds are often fried in oil or ghee (a cooking fat similar to clarified butter) to bring out their flavor before being combined with other ingredients.

1 Heat the oil in a large, heavy-bottom pan.

2 Add the white cumin seeds, mustard and onion seeds, and dried red chilies to the pan, stirring well.

3 Add the tomatoes to the pan and stir-fry the mixture for 3–5 minutes.

4 Mix the salt, ginger, garlic, and chili powder together in a bowl. Spoon the mixture into the pan and blend well.

5 Add the green beans and potatoes to the pan and stir-fry for 5 minutes.

6 Add the water, then reduce the heat and let simmer for 10–15 minutes, stirring occasionally.

7 Sprinkle over the chopped cilantro and chilies and serve.

potato curry

serves four

3 potatoes, peeled and rinsed
⅔ cup vegetable oil
1 tsp onion seeds
½ tsp fennel seeds
4 curry leaves
1 tsp ground cumin
1 tsp ground coriander
1 tsp chili powder
pinch of ground turmeric
1 tsp salt
1½ tsp amchoor (dried mango powder)

COOK'S TIP

Traditionally, Semolina Dessert (see page 248) is served to follow potato curry.

1 Using a sharp knife, cut each potato into 6 slices.

2 Boil the potato slices in a pan of water until just cooked, but not mushy (test by piercing with a sharp knife or a skewer). Drain and reserve until required.

3 Heat the oil in a separate pan. Reduce the heat and add the onion seeds, fennel seeds, and curry leaves, stirring to mix.

4 Remove the pan from the heat and add the cumin, ground coriander, chili powder, turmeric, salt, and amchoor. Stir well until mixed.

5 Return the pan to the heat and stir-fry the mixture for 1 minute.

6 Pour this mixture over the cooked potatoes and mix together, then stir-fry over low heat for 5 minutes.

7 Transfer the potato curry to warmed serving dishes and serve immediately.

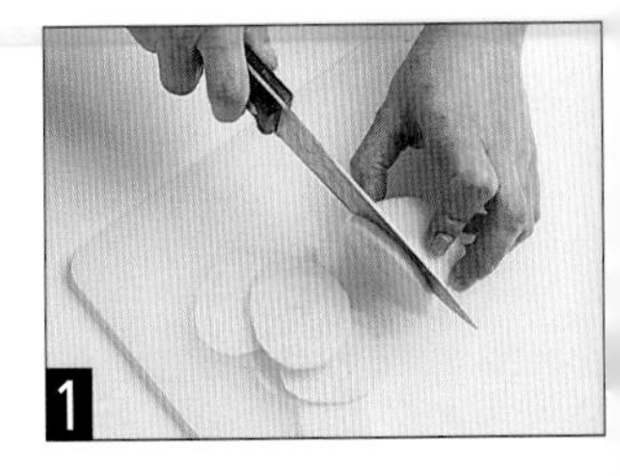

spinach & cheese curry

serves four

1¼ cups vegetable oil

7 oz/200 g paneer cheese, cubed (see Cook's Tip)

3 tomatoes, sliced

1 tsp ground cumin

1½ tsp ground chili powder

1 tsp salt

14 oz/400 g fresh spinach leaves

3 fresh green chilies

COOK'S TIP

To make paneer, boil 4 cups milk slowly over low heat, then add 2 tablespoons lemon juice, stirring constantly until the milk thickens and begins to curdle. Strain the milk and let stand under a heavy weight for 1½–2 hours to press to a flat shape about ½ inch/1 cm thick. Once set, the paneer can be cut into whatever shape is required. It is also available from Asian food stores.

1 Heat the oil in a large, heavy-bottom skillet. Add the cubed paneer and cook, stirring occasionally, until golden brown.

2 Add the tomatoes and stir-fry, breaking up the tomatoes, for 5 minutes.

3 Add the cumin, chili powder, and salt to the skillet and mix together well.

4 Add the spinach and stir-fry over low heat for 7–10 minutes.

5 Add the chilies and cook, stirring, for an additional 2 minutes.

6 Transfer to serving plates and serve hot.

vegetable patties

serves four

2 large potatoes, sliced

1 onion, sliced

½ cauliflower, cut into small florets

scant ½ cup peas

1 tbsp spinach purée

2–3 fresh green chilies

¼ bunch cilantro, chopped, plus extra to garnish

1 tsp finely chopped fresh gingerroot

1 garlic clove, crushed

1 tsp ground coriander

pinch of ground turmeric

1 tsp salt

scant 1 cup bread crumbs

1¼ cups vegetable oil

fresh chili strips, to garnish

1 Place the potatoes, onion, and cauliflower florets in a pan of water and bring to a boil. Reduce the heat and let simmer until the potatoes are cooked through. Remove the vegetables from the pan with a slotted spoon and drain thoroughly.

2 Add the peas and spinach purée to the vegetables and mix, mashing down with a fork.

3 Chop the chilies, then mix with the chopped cilantro, ginger, garlic, ground coriander, turmeric, and salt in a bowl.

4 Blend the spice mixture into the vegetables, mixing with a fork to make a paste. Spread the bread crumbs out on a large plate.

5 With dampened hands, divide the vegetable mixture into 10–12 small balls. Flatten them with the palm of your hands to make flat circles.

6 Dip each circle in the bread crumbs, coating well.

7 Heat the oil in a heavy-bottom skillet and shallow-fry the patties, in batches, until golden brown, turning occasionally. Transfer to serving plates and garnish with chili strips and extra cilantro. Serve hot.

balti vegetables

serves four

3 tbsp ghee or vegetable oil
1 onion, chopped
1 tsp Garlic Paste (see page 7)
1 tsp Ginger Paste (see page 7)
2 tsp ground coriander
1 tsp chili powder
½ tsp ground turmeric
½ cauliflower, broken into florets
2 potatoes, diced
2 carrots, diced
1 cup frozen peas, thawed
1 small rutabaga, diced
¾ cup green beans, cut into 2-inch/5-cm pieces
½ cup corn kernels, thawed if frozen
4 tomatoes, peeled and chopped
salt
4–8 tbsp vegetable stock or water
cilantro sprigs, to garnish

1 Heat the ghee in a large pan. Add the onion and cook over low heat, stirring occasionally, for 10 minutes, or until golden. Stir in the Garlic Paste and Ginger Paste and cook for 1 minute. Add the ground coriander, chili powder, and turmeric and cook, stirring, for 2 minutes, or until the spices give off their aroma.

2 Add the cauliflower, potatoes, carrots, peas, rutabaga, green beans, and corn and cook, stirring, for an additional 3 minutes. Add the tomatoes and salt to taste, then pour in 4 tablespoons of the stock.

3 Cover and simmer for 10 minutes, or until all the vegetables are tender. Check the mixture while it is cooking, and if the vegetables look as if they might catch on the base of the pan, add more stock. Serve, garnished with cilantro sprigs.

okra curry

serves four

1 lb/450 g okra

⅔ cup vegetable oil

2 onions, sliced

3 fresh green chilies, finely chopped

2 curry leaves

1 tsp salt

1 tomato, sliced

2 tbsp lemon juice

chopped cilantro

1 Rinse the okra and drain thoroughly. Using a sharp knife, chop and discard the ends. Cut the okra into 1-inch/2.5-cm long pieces.

COOK'S TIP

When you buy fresh okra, make sure they are not shriveled and that they do not have any brown spots. Fresh okra will keep, tightly wrapped, for up to 3 days in the refrigerator. Okra have a remarkable glutinous quality which naturally thickens curries and casseroles.

2 Heat the oil in a large, heavy-bottom skillet. Add the onions, chilies, curry leaves, and salt and mix together. Stir-fry the vegetables for 5 minutes.

3 Add the tomato to the skillet and sprinkle over the lemon juice.

4 Gradually add the okra, mixing in gently with a slotted spoon. Stir-fry the vegetable mixture over medium heat for 12–15 minutes.

5 Add the cilantro, then cover and let simmer for 3–5 minutes.

6 Transfer to serving plates and serve hot.

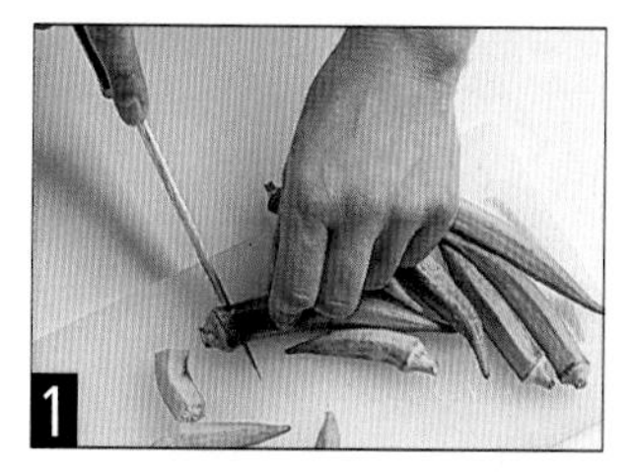

vegetable curry

serves four

8 oz/225 g turnips or rutabaga, peeled
1 eggplant, trimmed
12 oz /350 g new potatoes, scrubbed
8 oz/225 g cauliflower
8 oz/225 g white mushrooms
1 large onion
8 oz/225 g carrots, peeled
6 tbsp vegetable ghee or oil
2 garlic cloves, crushed
2-inch/5-cm piece fresh gingerroot, finely chopped
1–2 fresh green chilies, seeded and chopped
1 tbsp paprika
2 tsp ground coriander
1 tbsp mild or medium curry powder or paste
1¾ cups vegetable stock
2 cups canned chopped tomatoes
salt
1 green bell pepper, seeded and sliced
1 tbsp cornstarch
⅔ cup coconut milk
2–3 tbsp ground almonds
cilantro sprigs, to garnish

1 Cut the turnips, eggplant, and potatoes into ½-inch/1-cm cubes. Divide the cauliflower into small florets. Leave the mushrooms whole, or slice thickly if preferred. Slice the onion and carrots.

2 Heat the ghee in a large pan. Add the onion, carrots, turnip, potato, and cauliflower and cook gently for 3 minutes, stirring frequently. Add the garlic, ginger, chilies, paprika, ground coriander, and curry powder and cook for 1 minute, stirring constantly.

3 Add the stock, canned tomatoes, eggplant, and mushrooms and season with salt to taste. Cover and let simmer gently for 30 minutes or until tender, stirring occasionally. Add the green bell pepper, then cover and continue cooking for an additional 5 minutes.

4 Blend the cornstarch and coconut milk together until smooth. Stir into the mixture, then add the ground almonds and simmer for 2 minutes, stirring. Taste and adjust the seasoning if necessary. Serve hot, garnished with cilantro sprigs.

stuffed rice crêpes

serves six

1 cup rice and scant 1/4 cup urid dal, or 1 1/3 cups ground rice and 1/3 cup urid dal flour (ata)

2–2 1/2 cups water

1 tsp salt

4 tbsp vegetable oil

FILLING

4 potatoes, diced

3 fresh green chilies, chopped

1/2 tsp ground turmeric

1 tsp salt

2/3 cup vegetable oil

1 tsp mixed mustard and onion seeds

3 dried red chilies

4 curry leaves

2 tbsp lemon juice

1 To make the crêpes (dosas), soak the rice and urid dal for 3 hours. Grind the rice and urid dal to a smooth consistency, adding water if necessary. Let stand for an additional 3 hours to ferment. Alternatively, if you are using ground rice and urid dal flour, mix together in a bowl. Add the water and salt and stir until a batter is formed.

2 Heat 1 tablespoon of the oil in a large, nonstick skillet. Using a ladle, spoon the batter into the skillet. Tilt the skillet to spread the mixture over the base. Cover and cook over medium heat for 2 minutes. Remove the lid and turn the crêpes over very carefully. Pour a little oil around the edge, then cover and cook for an additional 2 minutes. Repeat with the remaining batter.

3 To make the filling, boil the potatoes in a pan of water. Add the chilies, turmeric, and salt and cook until the potatoes are soft enough to be lightly mashed.

4 Heat the oil in a pan. Add the mustard and onion seeds, dried red chilies, and curry leaves and cook for 1 minute. Pour the spice mixture over the mashed potatoes, then sprinkle over the lemon juice and mix well. Spoon the potato filling on one half of each crêpe and fold the other half over the filling. Serve hot.

2

eggplant curry

serves four

1½ oz/40 g dried tamarind, coarsely chopped
½ cup boiling water
2 large eggplants, sliced
salt
2 tbsp ghee or vegetable oil
3 onions, sliced
1 tsp Garlic Paste (see page 7)
1 tsp Ginger Paste (see page 7)
4 curry leaves
1 fresh green chili, seeded and finely chopped
2 fresh red chilies, seeded and finely chopped
1 tbsp ground coriander
2 tsp cumin seeds
2 tsp yellow mustard seeds
2 tbsp tomato paste
generous 2 cups canned coconut milk
3 tbsp chopped cilantro, plus extra to garnish

1 Place the dried tamarind in a bowl, then add the boiling water and stir. Let soak for 30 minutes. Meanwhile, place the eggplant slices in a colander, sprinkling each layer with salt. Let drain for 30 minutes.

2 Strain the tamarind into a bowl, pressing down on the pulp with the back of a wooden spoon. Discard the contents of the strainer. Rinse the eggplant slices under cold running water and pat dry with paper towels.

3 Heat the ghee in a large pan. Add the onions and cook over low heat, stirring occasionally, for 10 minutes, or until golden. Stir in the Garlic Paste and Ginger Paste and cook, stirring constantly, for 2 minutes. Add the curry leaves, green and red chilies, ground coriander, cumin and mustard seeds, and tomato paste and cook, stirring constantly, for 2 minutes, or until the spices give off their aroma.

4 Add the tamarind liquid and coconut milk and bring to a boil. Add the eggplant slices, then cover and simmer for 12–15 minutes, or until the eggplant is tender. Uncover the pan and simmer for an additional 5 minutes, or until the sauce has thickened. Stir in the chopped cilantro and sprinkle the extra chopped herb on top, then serve immediately.

COOK'S TIP

Most contemporary varieties of eggplant no longer need salting to remove the bitter juices. However, doing so stops the vegetable from becoming too soggy.

1

3

4

potatoes with spices & onions

serves four

- 6 tbsp vegetable oil
- 2 onions, finely chopped
- 1 tsp finely chopped fresh gingerroot
- 1 garlic clove, crushed
- 1 tsp chili powder
- 1½ tsp ground cumin
- 1½ tsp ground coriander
- 1 tsp salt
- 14 oz/400 g canned new potatoes
- 1 tbsp lemon juice

BAGHAAR

- 3 tbsp vegetable oil
- 3 dried red chilies
- ½ tsp onion seeds
- ½ tsp mustard seeds
- ½ tsp fenugreek seeds
- 1 fresh green chili, finely chopped, to garnish

1 Heat the oil in a large pan. Add the onions and cook, stirring, until golden brown. Reduce the heat, then add the ginger, garlic, chili powder, ground cumin, ground coriander, and salt and stir-fry for about 1 minute. Remove the pan from the heat and reserve until required.

2 Drain the water from the canned potatoes. Add the potatoes to the onion and spice mixture. Sprinkle over the lemon juice and mix well.

3 To make the baghaar, heat the oil in a separate pan. Add the red chilies, onion seeds, mustard seeds, and fenugreek seeds and cook until the seeds turn a shade darker. Remove the pan from the heat and pour over the potatoes.

4 Garnish with the chopped chili and serve immediately.

COOK'S TIP

You could also serve these as an unusual accompaniment to plain roast lamb or lamb chops.

potatoes & peas

serves two–four

- ⅔ cup vegetable oil
- 3 onions, sliced
- 1 garlic clove, crushed
- 1 tsp finely chopped fresh gingerroot
- 1 tsp chili powder
- ½ tsp ground turmeric
- 1 tsp salt
- 2 fresh green chilies, finely chopped
- 1⅓ cups water
- 3 potatoes
- 1 cup peas
- chopped cilantro, to garnish

1 Heat the oil in a large skillet. Add the onions and cook, stirring occasionally, until golden brown.

2 Mix the garlic, ginger, chili powder, turmeric, salt, and chilies together in a bowl. Add the spice mixture to the onions in the skillet.

3 Stir in ⅔ cup of the water, then cover and cook until the onions are cooked through.

4 Meanwhile, using a sharp knife, cut each potato into 6 slices.

5 Add the potato slices to the mixture in the skillet and stir-fry for 5 minutes.

6 Add the peas and the remaining ⅔ cup of the water to the pan, then cover and cook for 7–10 minutes. Transfer the potatoes and peas to serving plates and serve garnished with chopped cilantro.

1

2

3

COOK'S TIP

Turmeric is an aromatic root which is dried and ground to produce the distinctive bright yellow-orange powder used in many Indian dishes. It has a warm, aromatic smell and a full, somewhat musty taste.

fried cauliflower

serves four

4 tbsp vegetable oil

½ tsp onion seeds

½ tsp mustard seeds

½ tsp fenugreek seeds

4 dried red chilies

1 small cauliflower, cut into small florets

1 tsp salt

1 green bell pepper, seeded and diced

VARIATION

For a weekend feast or a special occasion, this dish looks great made with baby cauliflowers instead of florets. Peel off most of the outer leaves, leaving a few small leaves for decoration. Blanch the baby cauliflowers whole for 4 minutes, then cook as above.

COOK'S TIP

Onion seeds are small and black. They may be labeled as kalonji in Asian food stores. Onion seeds can be used instead of pepper, but have a spicier taste.

1 Heat the oil in a large, heavy-bottom pan.

2 Add the onion seeds, mustard seeds, fenugreek seeds, and the dried red chilies to the pan, stirring to mix.

3 Reduce the heat and gradually add the cauliflower and salt to the pan. Stir-fry for 7–10 minutes, coating the cauliflower in the spice mixture.

4 Add the bell pepper and stir-fry the mixture for 3–5 minutes.

5 Transfer the spicy fried cauliflower to a serving dish and serve hot.

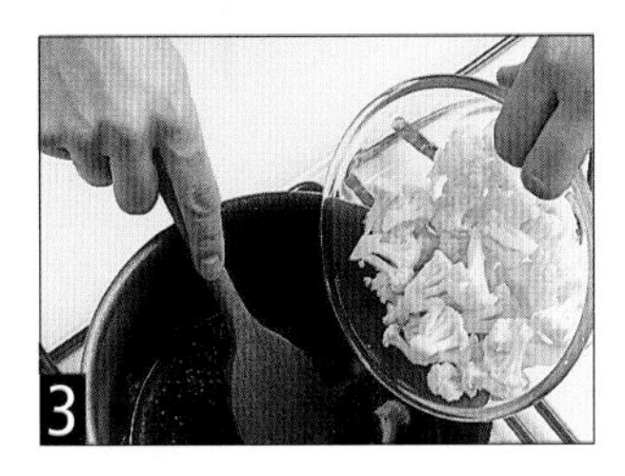

daikon curry

serves four

1 lb/450 g daikon, preferably with leaves

1 tbsp moong dal

1¼ cups water

⅔ cup vegetable oil

1 onion, thinly sliced

1 garlic clove, crushed

1 tsp dried chili flakes

1 tsp salt

Chapatis (see page 185), to serve

1 Rinse, then peel and slice the daikon, together with its leaves if wished.

2 Place the daikon, the leaves (if using), and the moong dal in a pan and pour over the water. Bring to a boil and cook until the daikon is soft.

3 Drain the daikon thoroughly, and use your hands to squeeze out any excess water.

4 Heat the oil in a pan. Add the onion, garlic, dried chili flakes, and salt and cook, stirring occasionally, until the onions have softened and turned a light golden brown color.

5 Stir the daikon mixture into the spiced onion mixture and mix well. Reduce the heat and continue cooking, stirring frequently, for 3–5 minutes.

6 Transfer the daikon curry to individual serving plates and serve hot with Chapatis.

COOK'S TIP

Daikon looks a bit like a parsnip without the tapering end and is now sold in many supermarkets as well as in Asian grocery stores.

kashmiri vegetables

serves four

3 tbsp ghee or vegetable oil
2 tbsp slivered almonds
8 cardamom seeds
8 black peppercorns
2 tsp cumin seeds
1 cinnamon stick
2 fresh green chilies, seeded and chopped
1 tsp Ginger Paste (see page 7)
1 tsp chili powder
3 potatoes, cut into chunks
salt
8 oz/225 g okra cut into 1-inch/2.5-cm pieces
½ cauliflower, broken into florets
⅔ cup plain yogurt
⅔ cup vegetable stock or water
freshly cooked rice, to serve

1 Heat 1 tablespoon of the ghee in a heavy-bottom pan. Add the almonds and cook over low heat, stirring constantly, for 2 minutes, or until golden.

2 Remove the almonds from the pan with a slotted spoon and drain on paper towels, then reserve. Place the cardamom seeds, peppercorns, cumin seeds, and cinnamon stick in a spice grinder or mortar and grind finely.

3 Add the remaining ghee to the pan and heat. Add the chilies and cook, stirring frequently, for 2 minutes. Stir in the Ginger Paste, chili powder, and ground spices and cook, stirring constantly, for 2 minutes, or until they give off their aroma.

4 Add the potatoes and season with salt to taste, then cover and cook, stirring occasionally, for 8 minutes. Add the okra and cauliflower and cook for an additional 5 minutes.

5 Gradually stir in the yogurt and stock and bring to a boil. Cover and simmer for an additional 10 minutes, or until all the vegetables are tender. Garnish with the almonds and serve with freshly cooked rice.

3

4

VARIATION

Use sweet potatoes instead of ordinary potatoes to give the dish a delicately sweet flavor.

eggplants & yogurt

serves four

2 eggplants
4 tbsp vegetable oil
1 onion, sliced
1 tsp white cumin seeds
1 tsp chili powder
1 tsp salt
3 tbsp plain yogurt
½ tsp mint sauce
fresh mint leaves, shredded, to garnish

1 Preheat the oven to 325°F/160°C. Rinse the eggplants and pat dry with paper towels.

2 Place the eggplants in an ovenproof dish. Bake in the preheated oven for 45 minutes. Remove the baked eggplants from the oven and let cool.

3 Slice the eggplants in half, then, using a spoon, scoop out the eggplant flesh and reserve. Heat the oil in a heavy-bottom pan. Add the onion and cumin seeds and cook, stirring, for 1–2 minutes.

4 Add the chili powder, salt, yogurt, and mint sauce to the pan and stir well to mix.

5 Add the eggplants to the onion and yogurt mixture and stir-fry for 5–7 minutes, or until all of the liquid has been absorbed and the mixture is quite dry.

6 Transfer the eggplant and yogurt mixture to a serving dish and garnish with mint leaves.

tomato curry

serves four

- 2 cups canned tomatoes
- 1 tsp finely chopped fresh gingerroot
- 1 garlic clove, crushed
- 1 tsp chili powder
- 1 tsp salt
- ½ tsp ground coriander
- ½ tsp ground cumin
- 4 tbsp vegetable oil
- ½ tsp onion seeds
- ½ tsp mustard seeds
- ½ tsp fenugreek seeds
- pinch of white cumin seeds
- 3 dried red chilies
- 2 tbsp lemon juice
- 3 hard-cooked eggs
- ¼ bunch of cilantro, chopped

1 Place the tomatoes in a large bowl. Add the ginger, garlic, chili powder, salt, ground coriander, and cumin to the tomatoes and blend well. Heat the oil in a pan. Add the onion, mustard, fenugreek and white cumin seeds, and the dried red chilies, and stir-fry for 1 minute. Remove the pan from the heat.

1

1

2

2 Add the tomato mixture to the spicy oil mixture and return to the heat. Stir-fry the mixture for 3 minutes, then reduce the heat and cook with the lid ajar for 7–10 minutes, stirring occasionally.

3 Sprinkle over the lemon juice. Transfer the tomato curry to a serving dish and keep warm until required.

4 Shell and quarter the hard-cooked eggs, then gently add them, yolk-end down, to the tomato curry.

5 Garnish with chopped cilantro and serve hot.

COOK'S TIP

This tomato curry can be made in advance and frozen, because it freezes particularly well.

eggplants in pickling spices

serves four

2 tsp ground coriander
2 tsp ground cumin
2 tsp dry unsweetened coconut
2 tsp sesame seeds
1 tsp mixed mustard and onion seeds
1¼ cups vegetable oil
3 onions, sliced
1 tsp chopped fresh gingerroot
1 garlic clove, crushed
½ tsp ground turmeric
1½ tsp chili powder
1½ tsp salt
3 eggplants, halved lengthwise
1 tbsp tamarind paste
1¼ cups water

BAGHAAR
⅔ cup vegetable oil
1 tsp mixed onion and mustard seeds
1 tsp cumin seeds
4 dried red chilies
3 tbsp finely chopped cilantro
1 fresh green chili, finely chopped

TO GARNISH
3 hard-cooked eggs, cut into fourths
cilantro sprigs

1 Dry-roast the ground coriander, cumin, coconut, sesame seeds, and mustard and onion seeds in a pan. Using a pestle and mortar, grind briefly. Alternatively, use a food processor. Heat the oil in a skillet. Add the onions and cook until golden. Reduce the heat and add the ginger, garlic, turmeric, chili powder, and salt, stirring. Let cool, then grind this mixture to form a paste.

1

1

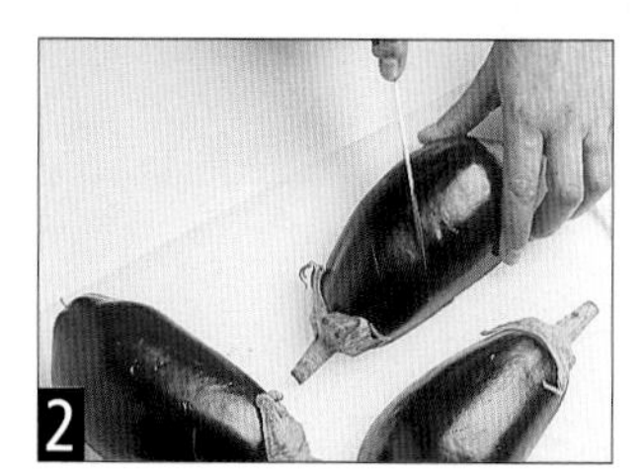
2

2 Make 4 cuts across each eggplant half. Blend the spices with the onion paste. Spoon this mixture into the slits in the eggplants.

3 Mix the tamarind paste and 3 tablespoons of the water together to make a paste. Reserve.

4 For the baghaar, heat the oil in a large skillet. Add the onion and mustard seeds, cumin seeds, and chilies and cook briefly. Reduce the heat, then gently place the stuffed eggplants into the baghaar and stir gently. Stir in the tamarind paste and the remaining water and cook for 15–20 minutes. Add the cilantro and chili. When cool, transfer to a serving dish and serve garnished with the hard-cooked eggs and cilantro sprigs.

dumplings in yogurt sauce

serves four

$\frac{2}{3}$ cup besan
1 tsp chili powder
$\frac{1}{2}$ tsp salt
$\frac{1}{2}$ tsp baking soda
1 onion, finely chopped
2 fresh green chilies, chopped
$\frac{1}{4}$ bunch of cilantro, chopped
$\frac{2}{3}$ cup water
$1\frac{1}{4}$ cups vegetable oil

YOGURT SAUCE
$1\frac{1}{4}$ cups plain yogurt
3 tbsp besan
$\frac{2}{3}$ cup water
1 tsp chopped fresh gingerroot
1 garlic clove, crushed
$1\frac{1}{2}$ tsp chili powder
$1\frac{1}{2}$ tsp salt
$\frac{1}{2}$ tsp ground turmeric
1 tsp ground coriander
1 tsp ground cumin

BAGHAAR
$\frac{2}{3}$ cup vegetable oil
1 tsp white cumin seeds
6 dried red chilies

1 To make the dumplings, sift the besan into a large bowl. Add the chili powder, salt, baking soda, onion, chopped chilies, and cilantro and mix. Add the water and mix to make a thick paste. Heat the oil in a skillet. Place teaspoonfuls of the paste in the oil and cook, turning once, over medium heat until a crisp golden brown. Reserve.

1

2 To make the sauce, place the yogurt in a bowl and whisk in the besan and water. Add all of the spices and mix well.

2

3 Push this mixture through a large strainer into a pan. Bring to a boil over low heat, stirring constantly. If the yogurt sauce becomes too thick, add a little extra water.

4 Pour the sauce into a deep serving dish and arrange all of the dumplings on top. Keep warm.

5 To make the baghaar, heat the oil in a skillet. Add the cumin seeds and the dried red chilies and cook until darker in color. Pour the dressing over the dumplings and serve hot.

stuffed bell peppers

serves four

scant ½ cup vegetable oil

1 onion, finely chopped

1 potato, diced

½ cup peas, thawed if frozen

½ cup fava beans

2 oz/55 g small cauliflower florets

scant ½ cup carrot, diced

½ cup corn kernels

2 tsp amchoor (dried mango powder)

1 tsp Garam Masala (see page 7)

½ tsp chili powder

salt

4 large or 8 small green bell peppers

VARIATION

Substitute other vegetables in the filling, such as broccoli, chopped mushrooms, diced zucchini, and eggplant.

1 Preheat the oven to 325°F/160°C. Heat 4 tablespoons of the vegetable oil in a heavy-bottom pan. Add the onion and cook over low heat, stirring occasionally, for 5 minutes, or until softened. Add the potato and cook, stirring occasionally, for an additional 5 minutes.

2 Add the peas, fava beans, cauliflower, carrot, corn, amchoor, Garam Masala, and chili powder and season with salt to taste. Stir well, then cover and cook for 15 minutes, or until all the vegetables are tender. Remove the pan from the heat and let cool.

3 Cut the tops off the bell peppers to make "lids," then seed. Heat the remaining vegetable oil in a skillet and cook the bell peppers, turning frequently, for 3 minutes. Remove with a slotted spoon and drain on paper towels. Spoon the vegetable mixture into the bell peppers and arrange them in a single layer in an ovenproof dish. Bake in the preheated oven for 20 minutes, then serve immediately.

COOK'S TIP

Chili powder is made from dried red chilies and is usually very hot, so use with caution. It is available from most large supermarkets.

chickpea curry

serves four

6 tbsp vegetable oil
2 onions, sliced
1 tsp finely chopped fresh gingerroot
1 tsp ground cumin
1 tsp ground coriander
1 garlic clove, crushed
1 tsp chili powder
2 fresh green chilies
½ bunch of cilantro, chopped
⅔ cup water
1 large potato
1½ cups canned chickpeas, drained
1 tbsp lemon juice

COOK'S TIP

Using canned chickpeas saves time, but you can use dried chickpeas if you prefer. Soak them overnight, then boil them for 15–20 minutes, or until soft.

1 Heat the oil in a large pan. Add the onions and cook, stirring occasionally, until golden brown.

2

2

2 Reduce the heat, then add the ginger, ground cumin, ground coriander, garlic, chili powder, green chilies, and chopped cilantro to the pan and stir-fry for 2 minutes.

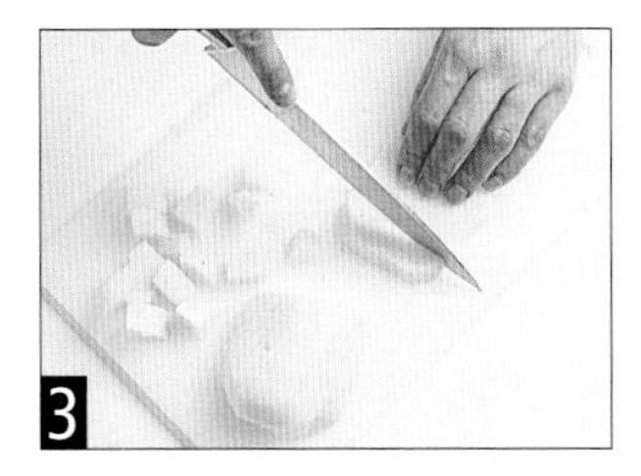
3

3 Add the water to the mixture in the pan and stir to mix. Peel and dice the potato.

4 Add the diced potato and the drained chickpeas to the mixture in the pan, then cover and let simmer, stirring occasionally, for 5–7 minutes.

5 Sprinkle the lemon juice over the curry.

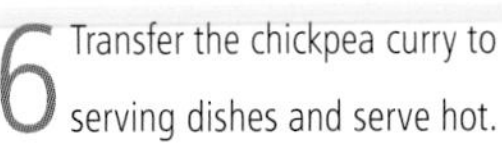

6 Transfer the chickpea curry to serving dishes and serve hot.

potato & cauliflower curry

serves four

- ⅔ cup vegetable oil
- ½ tsp white cumin seeds
- 4 dried red chilies
- 2 onions, sliced
- 1 tsp finely chopped fresh gingerroot
- 1 garlic clove, crushed
- 1 tsp chili powder
- 1 tsp salt
- pinch of ground turmeric
- 3 potatoes
- ½ cauliflower, cut into small florets
- 2 fresh green chilies (optional)
- ¼ bunch of cilantro, chopped
- ⅔ cup water

COOK'S TIP

Always handle chilies with caution, preferably wearing rubber gloves, because the juices are extremely pungent. Wash your hands thoroughly after preparing and handling chilies and do not put your fingers near your eyes, as this can be very painful.

1 Heat the oil in a large pan. Add the white cumin seeds and dried red chilies, stirring to mix.

2 Add the onions to the pan and cook, stirring occasionally, until golden brown.

3 Mix the ginger, garlic, chili powder, salt, and turmeric together in a bowl. Add the spice mixture to the onions and stir-fry for 2 minutes.

4 Add the potatoes and cauliflower to the onion and spice mixture, stirring to coat the vegetables in the spice mixture.

5 Reduce the heat and add the green chilies (if using), cilantro, and water to the pan. Cover and let simmer for 10–15 minutes.

6 Transfer the potato and cauliflower curry to warmed serving plates and serve immediately.

1

2

3

green pumpkin curry

serves four

- ⅔ cup vegetable oil
- 2 onions, sliced
- ½ tsp white cumin seeds
- 1 lb/450 g green pumpkin, cubed
- 1 tsp amchoor (dried mango powder)
- 1 tsp finely chopped fresh gingerroot
- 1 garlic clove, crushed
- 1 tsp dried chili flakes
- ½ tsp salt
- 1¼ cups water

1. Heat the oil in a large skillet. Add the onions and cumin seeds and cook, stirring occasionally, until a light golden brown color.

2. Add the cubed pumpkin to the skillet and stir-fry for 3–5 minutes over low heat.

3. Mix the amchoor, ginger, garlic, dried chili flakes, and salt together in a bowl.

COOK'S TIP

Cumin seeds are popular in Indian cooking because of their warm, pungent flavor and aroma. The seeds are sold whole or ground, and are included as one of the flavorings in Garam Masala (see page 7).

VARIATION

You can use ordinary pumpkin for this recipe, if you prefer.

4. Add the spice mixture to the pumpkin mixture, stirring well to mix.

5. Add the water, then cover and cook over low heat for 10–15 minutes, stirring occasionally.

6. Transfer to warmed serving plates and serve hot.

stuffed eggplants

serves four

2 large eggplants

2 carrots, diced

2 potatoes, diced

2 zucchini, diced

⅔ cup vegetable stock
or ½ vegetable stock cube
dissolved in ⅔ cup hot water

½ tsp ground coriander

½ tsp ground cumin, plus extra
for sprinkling

½ tsp ground cardamom

½ tsp ground turmeric

¼ tsp ground cinnamon

¼ tsp cayenne pepper

¼ tsp ground cloves

¼ tsp ground mace

1 onion, thinly sliced

salt

1 tbsp chopped fresh mint

fresh mint sprigs, to garnish

COOK'S TIP

This is a terrific recipe for anyone following a lowfat eating plan, because steaming and simmering the vegetables is a healthy way of cooking.

1 Preheat the oven to 375°F/190°C. Halve the eggplants lengthwise and, using a sharp knife, cut all around the edges without piercing the skins. Cut a crisscross pattern in the flesh and carefully scoop out with a spoon, leaving the shells intact. Steam the shells over a pan of boiling water for 5 minutes, or until tender, but not disintegrating. Remove and let cool. Place the carrots and potatoes in the steamer and cook for 3 minutes, then add the zucchini and cook for an additional 3 minutes. Transfer the vegetables to a bowl.

2 Chop the eggplant flesh. Bring the stock to a boil in a pan. Stir in the coriander, cumin, cardamom, turmeric, cinnamon, cayenne, cloves, and mace and add the onion. Simmer, stirring occasionally, for 5 minutes. Add the eggplant flesh and simmer for an additional 5 minutes. Stir in the carrots, potatoes, and zucchini, then add salt to taste and remove the pan from the heat. Add the mint.

3 Arrange the eggplant shells in a single layer in an ovenproof dish. Divide the vegetable mixture between them and sprinkle very lightly with a little extra ground cumin. Cover with foil and bake in the preheated oven for 30 minutes, or until tender. Serve garnished with mint sprigs.

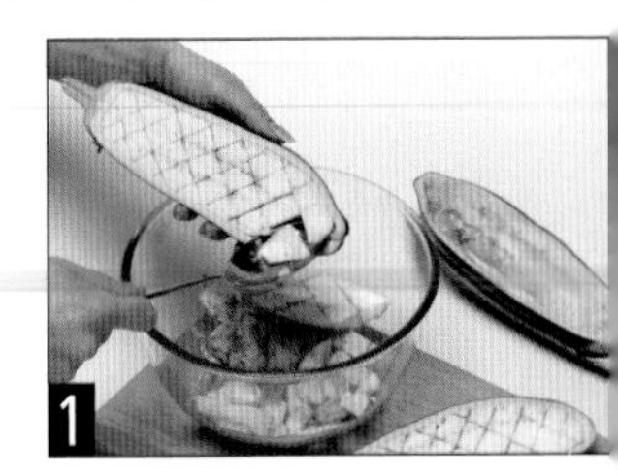

egg curry

serves four

4 tbsp vegetable oil

1 onion, sliced

1 red chili, finely chopped

½ tsp chili powder

½ tsp finely chopped fresh gingerroot

1–2 garlic cloves, crushed

4 eggs

1 firm tomato, sliced

¼ bunch of cilantro, chopped, to garnish

1 Heat the oil in a large pan. Add the onion and cook until just softened and a light golden color.

2 Add the chili, chili powder, ginger, and garlic and stir-fry over low heat for 1 minute.

3 Add the eggs and tomato slices to the mixture in the pan and continue cooking, stirring to break up the eggs when they begin to cook, for 3–5 minutes.

4 Sprinkle over the chopped cilantro. Transfer the egg curry to serving plates and serve hot.

COOK'S TIP

Eggs contain high quality protein, fat, iron, and vitamins A, B, and D, although they are also high in cholesterol. Both the leaves and finely chopped stems of cilantro are used in Indian cooking, to flavor dishes and as edible garnishes. Cilantro has a very distinctive and pronounced taste.

mixed vegetables

serves four

1¼ cups vegetable oil
1 tsp mustard seeds
1 tsp onion seeds
½ tsp white cumin seeds
3–4 curry leaves, chopped
1 lb/450 g onions, finely chopped
3 tomatoes, chopped
½ red and ½ green bell pepper, seeded and sliced
1 tsp finely chopped fresh gingerroot
1 garlic clove, crushed
1 tsp chili powder
¼ tsp ground turmeric
1 tsp salt
1¾ cups water
2 potatoes, peeled and cut into pieces
½ cauliflower, cut into small florets
4 carrots, peeled and sliced
3 fresh green chilies, finely chopped
¼ bunch of cilantro, finely chopped
1 tbsp lemon juice
freshly cooked rice, to serve

1 Heat the oil in a large pan. Add the mustard, onion, and cumin seeds along with the curry leaves and cook until they turn a shade darker.

2 Add the onions to the pan and cook over medium heat until golden brown.

3 Add the tomatoes and bell peppers and stir-fry for 5 minutes.

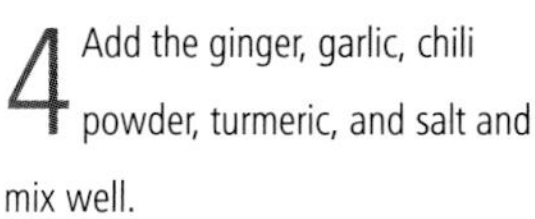

4 Add the ginger, garlic, chili powder, turmeric, and salt and mix well.

5 Add 1¼ cups of the water, then cover and let simmer for 10–12 minutes, stirring occasionally. Add the potatoes, cauliflower, carrots, green chilies, and cilantro and stir-fry for 5 minutes.

6 Add the remaining water and the lemon juice, stirring well. Cover and let simmer for 15 minutes, stirring occasionally.

7 Transfer the mixed vegetables to warmed serving plates and serve immediately with rice.

zucchini & fenugreek seeds

serves four

6 tbsp vegetable oil

1 onion, finely chopped

3 fresh green chilies, finely chopped

1 tsp finely chopped fresh gingerroot

1 garlic clove, crushed

1 tsp chili powder

1 lb/450 g zucchini, sliced

2 tomatoes, sliced

2 tsp fenugreek seeds

chopped cilantro, to garnish

Chapatis (see page 185), to serve

1 Heat the oil in a large, heavy-bottom skillet. Add the onion, green chilies, ginger, garlic, and chili powder, stirring well until mixed.

1

2 Add the sliced zucchini and tomatoes to the skillet and stir-fry for 5–7 minutes.

2

3 Add the fenugreek seeds to the zucchini mixture in the skillet and stir-fry for an additional 5 minutes.

2

4 Remove the skillet from the heat and transfer the zucchini and fenugreek seed mixture to serving dishes. Garnish with cilantro and serve hot with Chapatis.

COOK'S TIP

Fresh fenugreek is sold in bunches. Both the leaves and the flat, yellowish-brown seeds are used, but the stems and root should be discarded, because they have a bitter taste.

dry split okra

serves four

1 lb/450 g okra
⅔ cup vegetable oil
3½ oz/100 g dried onions
2 tsp amchoor (dried mango powder)
1 tsp ground cumin
1 tsp chili powder
1 tsp salt

1 Trim the ends off the okra, then carefully split down the center without cutting through completely.

2 Heat the oil in a large pan. Add the dried onions and cook until crisp.

3 Remove the onions from the pan with a slotted spoon and let drain thoroughly on paper towels.

4 When cool enough to handle, coarsely tear the dried onions and place in a large bowl.

COOK'S TIP

Amchoor is made from dried ground mangoes. It has a slightly sour taste. Amchoor is sold in jars from specialty Asian food stores.

5 Add the amchoor, ground cumin, chili powder, and salt to the dried onions and blend well.

6 Spoon the onion and spice mixture into the split okra.

7 Reheat the oil in the pan. Gently add the okra to the hot oil and cook over low heat for 10–12 minutes.

8 Transfer the cooked okra to a warmed serving dish and serve immediately.

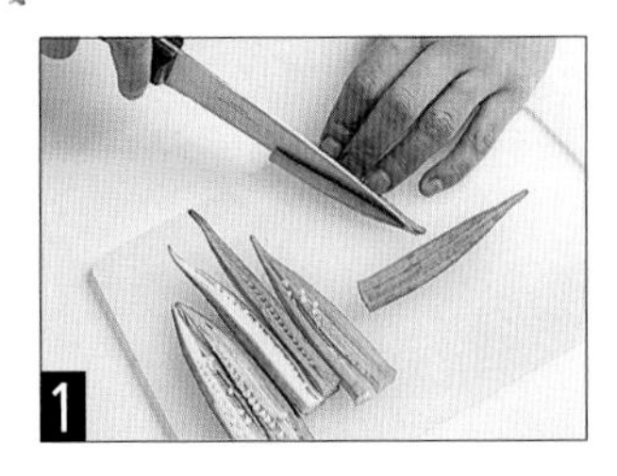
1

2

5

Bread, Beans & Grains

The most common Indian breads are chapatis, parathas, and pooris and are cooked almost every day in most Indian households. They are made as individual portions, and you should allow for 2 per person.

Rice is served with almost every meal in India, so the Indians have created a variety of ways of cooking it. Whatever the dish, the aim is to produce dry, separate grains of rice that are cooked yet still have some "bite" to them. Basmati rice is the best choice, because it cooks very well and gives an excellent result.

There are at least 30 different types of lentil to be found in India, but the most commonly used ones are moong, masoor, chana, and urid. Rich in protein, lentils make ideal accompaniments to vegetable curries. Lentils are also delicious cooked with a variety of meats.

lemon dal

serves four

scant ½ cup masoor dal
1 tsp finely chopped fresh gingerroot
1 garlic clove, crushed
1 tsp chili powder
½ tsp ground turmeric
1¾ cups water
1 tsp salt
3 tbsp lemon juice
2 fresh green chilies
¼ bunch of cilantro, chopped

BAGHAAR
⅔ cup vegetable oil
4 whole garlic cloves
6 dried red chilies
1 tsp white cumin seeds
1 lemon, cut into slices, to garnish

1 Rinse the dal twice under cold running water, removing any stones. Place in a large pan.

2 Add the ginger, garlic, chili powder, and turmeric to the dal. Stir in 1¼ cups of the water and bring to a boil over a medium heat with the lid left slightly ajar. Cook for 30 minutes, or until the dal is soft enough to be mashed.

3 Remove the pan from the heat and mash the dal with a potato masher. Add the salt, lemon juice, and remaining water, then stir and mix well. It should be a fairly smooth consistency.

4 Seed and finely chop the green chilies, then add to the pan with the cilantro and keep warm.

5 To make the baghaar, heat the oil in a pan. Add the garlic, red chilies, and cumin seeds and cook for 1 minute. Turn off the heat, and when the heat has been reduced pour the baghaar over the dal. If the dal is too runny, cook, uncovered, over medium heat for 3–5 minutes.

6 Transfer the dal to a serving dish and garnish with lemon slices. Serve hot.

COOK'S TIP

This dish is a good accompaniment to Beef Korma with Almonds (see page 56).

strained dal with meatballs

serves six–eight

scant 1 cup masoor dal
3¾ cups water
1 tsp finely chopped fresh gingerroot
1 garlic clove, crushed
½ tsp ground turmeric
1½ tsp chili powder
1½ tsp salt
3 tbsp lemon juice
Beef Patties (see page 55)

BAGHAAR
⅔ cups vegetable oil
3 whole garlic cloves
4 dried red chilies
1 tsp white cumin seeds

POTATO WAFERS
pinch of salt
2 potatoes, cut into shavings
1¼ cups vegetable oil

TO GARNISH
3 fresh green chilies, finely chopped
¼ bunch of cilantro, chopped

1 Rinse the dal twice under cold running water, removing any stones. Place the dal in a pan and cover with 2½ cups of the water. Add the ginger, garlic, turmeric, and chili powder and boil for 20 minutes, or until the dal is soft and mushy. Add the salt, stirring.

2 Remove the pan from the heat and mash the dal with a potato masher, then push it through a strainer. Add the lemon juice and stir in the remaining water. Transfer to a clean pan and bring to a boil over low heat. Reserve.

3 To make the meatballs, follow the recipe for Beef Patties on page 55, but shape into small balls rather than flat circles. Drop the meatballs gently into the dal mixture and keep warm.

4 Prepare the baghaar. Heat the oil in a pan. Add the garlic, dried red chilies, and cumin seeds and cook for 2 minutes. Pour the baghaar over the dal mixture, stirring to mix.

5 For the potato wafers, rub the salt over the potato shavings. Heat the oil in a skillet. Add the potatoes and cook, turning occasionally, until crisp. Garnish the meatballs with the potato wafers, chilies, and chopped cilantro.

1

2

2

black-eye peas

serves four

scant 1 cup dried black-eye peas

1¼ cups vegetable oil

2 onions, sliced

1 tsp finely chopped fresh gingerroot

1 garlic clove, crushed

1 tsp chili powder

1½ tsp salt

1½ tsp ground coriander

1½ tsp ground cumin

⅔ cup water

2 fresh red chilies, cut into strips

½ bunch of cilantro, chopped

1 tbsp lemon juice

1 Rinse the black-eye peas under cold running water, then soak in a bowl of water overnight.

2 Place the black-eye peas in a pan of water and bring to a boil, then cook over low heat for 30 minutes. Drain the beans thoroughly and reserve.

3 Heat the oil in a separate pan. Add the onions and cook until golden brown. Add the ginger, garlic, chili powder, salt, ground coriander, and ground cumin and stir-fry the mixture for 3–5 minutes.

4 Add the water to the pan, then cover and cook until all of the water has completely evaporated.

5 Add the boiled black-eye peas, red chilies and cilantro to the beans and stir to blend together. Stir-fry the bean mixture for 3–5 minutes.

6 Transfer the black-eye peas to a serving dish and sprinkle over the lemon juice. Serve hot or cold.

2

3

4

COOK'S TIP

Black-eye peas are oval-shaped, gray or beige beans with a dark dot in the center. They have a slightly smoky flavor and are sold canned as well as dried.

white lentils

serves two–four

- scant ½ cup urid dal
- 1 tsp finely chopped fresh gingerroot
- 2½ cups water
- 1 tsp salt
- 1 tsp coarsely ground pepper
- 2 tbsp ghee
- 2 garlic cloves, peeled but kept whole
- 2 fresh red chilies, finely chopped
- fresh mint leaves, to garnish

1 Rinse the dal twice under cold water, removing any stones.

2 Place the dal and ginger in a large pan.

3 Add the water, then cover and bring to a boil. Cook over medium heat for 30 minutes. Check to see whether the dal is cooked by rubbing it between your forefinger and thumb. If the dal is a little hard in the center, cook for an additional 5–7 minutes. If necessary, remove the lid and cook until any remaining water has evaporated.

4 Add the salt and pepper to the dal and mix well, then reserve.

5 Heat the ghee in a separate pan. Add the garlic cloves and red chilies, and stir well to mix.

6 Pour the garlic and chili mixture over the dal and garnish with the mint leaves.

7 Transfer the white lentils to serving dishes and serve hot.

3

3

4

dry moong dal

serves four

scant ¾ cup moong dal
1 tsp finely chopped fresh gingerroot
½ tsp ground cumin
½ tsp ground coriander
1 garlic clove, crushed
½ tsp chili powder
2½ cups water
1 tsp salt
BAGHAAR
scant ½ cup unsalted butter
5 dried red chilies
1 tsp white cumin seeds

1 Rinse the dal twice under cold running water, removing any stones.

2 Place the dal in a pan. Add the ginger, ground cumin, ground coriander, garlic, and chili powder and stir to mix.

3 Pour in the water to cover the dal mixture. Cook over medium heat, stirring, for 20 minutes,or until the dal is soft but not mushy.

4 Add the salt and stir to mix. Transfer to a serving dish and keep warm.

5 Meanwhile, make the baghaar. Melt the butter in a pan. Add the dried red chilies and cumin seeds and cook until they begin to pop.

6 Pour the baghaar over the dal and serve hot.

COOK'S TIP

Dried red chilies are the quickest way to add heat to a dish.

chana dal cooked with rice

serves six

scant ½ cup chana dal
2¼ cups basmati rice
4 tbsp ghee
2 onions, sliced
1 tsp finely chopped fresh gingerroot
1 garlic clove, crushed
½ tsp ground turmeric
2 tsp salt
½ tsp chili powder
1 tsp Garam Masala (see page 7)
5 tbsp plain yogurt
5 cups water
⅔ cup milk
1 tsp saffron threads
3 black cardamoms
3 black cumin seeds
3 tbsp lemon juice
2 fresh green chilies
¼ bunch of cilantro, chopped

1 Rinse the dal twice under cold running water, removing any stones, then soak in a bowl of water for 3 hours. Rinse the rice and reserve.

2 Heat the ghee in a skillet. Add the onions and cook until golden brown. Using a slotted spoon, remove half of the onion with a little of the ghee and place in a bowl.

2

3

5

3 Add the ginger, garlic, turmeric, 1 teaspoon of the salt, the chili powder, and Garam Masala to the mixture remaining in the skillet and stir-fry for 5 minutes. Stir in the yogurt and add the dal and ⅔ cup of the water. Cook, covered, for 15 minutes. Reserve.

4 Meanwhile, boil the milk with the saffron and reserve.

5 Boil the remaining water and add the remaining salt, cardamoms, cumin seeds, and the rice, and cook, stirring, until the rice is half cooked. Drain, and place half of the following ingredients—fried onion, saffron milk, lemon juice, green chilies, and cilantro—on top of the dal mixture. Place the remaining rice on top of this and the rest of the fried onion, saffron milk, lemon juice, chilies, and cilantro on top of the rice. Cover tightly with a lid and cook for 20 minutes over very low heat. Mix with a slotted spoon before serving.

onion dal

serves four

scant ½ cup masoor dal
6 tbsp vegetable oil
1 small bunch of scallions, trimmed and chopped, including the green part
1 tsp finely chopped fresh gingerroot
1 garlic clove, crushed
½ tsp chili powder
½ tsp ground turmeric
1¼ cups water
1 tsp salt
TO GARNISH
1 fresh green chili, finely chopped
¼ bunch of cilantro, chopped

1 Rinse the dal twice, removing any stones and reserve.

2 Heat the oil in a pan. Add the scallions and cook until lightly browned.

3 Reduce the heat and add the ginger, garlic, chili powder, and turmeric to the pan. Stir-fry the scallions with the spices.

4 Add the dal and mix to blend together.

5 Add the water to the dal mixture in the pan, then reduce the heat further and cook for 20–25 minutes.

6 When the dal is cooked thoroughly, add the salt and stir gently with a wooden spoon to mix.

7 Transfer the onion dal to a serving dish and garnish with the chopped green chili and cilantro. Serve immediately.

fried spicy rice

serves four–six

2½ cups basmati rice
1 onion
2 tbsp ghee
1 tsp finely chopped fresh gingerroot
1 garlic clove, crushed
1 tsp salt
1 tsp black cumin seeds
3 cloves
3 green cardamoms
2 cinnamon sticks
4 peppercorns
3 cups water

1 Rinse the rice thoroughly under cold running water.

2 Slice the onion. Melt the ghee in a large skillet. Add the onion and cook until a crisp golden brown color.

3 Add the ginger, garlic, and salt to the skillet, stirring to mix.

4 Add the rice, cumin seeds, cloves, cardamoms, cinnamon sticks, and peppercorns to the mixture in the skillet and stir-fry for 3–5 minutes.

COOK'S TIP

Cardamom pods contain numerous tiny black seeds which have a warm flavor and are highly aromatic—green cardamoms are considered the best because of their fine delicate flavor. Green cardamoms are also prized for their digestive properties, and some Indians chew them raw after they have eaten extra-spicy curries, to aid digestion and sweeten the breath.

5 Add the water and bring to a boil. Reduce the heat, then cover and cook until the rice is tender.

6 Drain the fried spicy rice and transfer to a serving dish. Serve immediately.

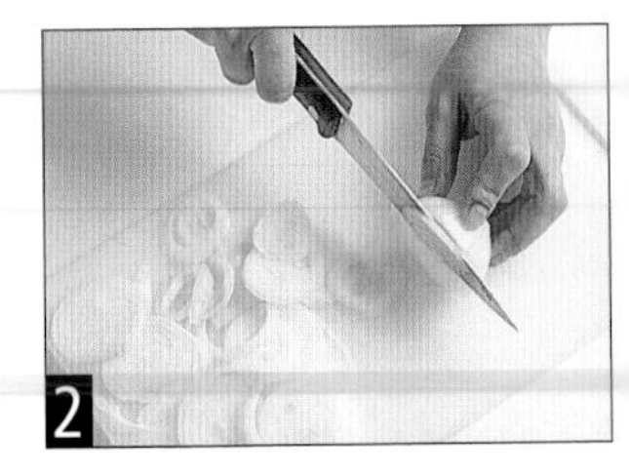

2

3

4

spinach & chana dal

serves four–six

- 4 tbsp chana dal
- 6 tbsp vegetable oil
- 1 tsp mixed onion and mustard seeds
- 4 dried red chilies
- 14–16 oz/400–450 g canned spinach, drained
- 1 tsp finely chopped fresh gingerroot
- 1 tsp ground coriander
- 1 tsp ground cumin
- 1 tsp salt
- 1 tsp chili powder
- 2 tbsp lemon juice
- 1 fresh green chili, to garnish

1 Rinse the lentils twice under cold running water, then soak in a bowl of warm water for at least 3 hours, preferably overnight.

COOK'S TIP

Very similar in appearance to moong dal—the yellow split peas—chana dal has slightly less shiny grains. It is used as a binding agent and can be bought from Asian food stores.

2 Place the lentils in a pan, then cover with water and boil for 30 minutes.

3 Heat the oil in a pan. Add the onion and mustard seeds and dried red chilies and cook, stirring, until they turn a shade darker.

4 Add the drained spinach to the pan, mixing gently.

5 Add the root ginger, ground coriander, cumin, salt, and chili powder to the pan. Reduce the heat and gently stir-fry the mixture for 7–10 minutes.

6 Add the dal to the pan and blend into the spinach mixture well, stirring gently so that it does not break up.

7 Transfer the mixture to a serving dish. Sprinkle over the lemon juice and garnish with the green chili. Serve immediately.

oil-dressed dal

serves four

generous ¼ cup masoor dal

scant ¼ cup moong dal

1¾ cups water

1 tsp finely chopped fresh gingerroot

1 garlic clove, crushed

2 fresh red chilies, chopped

1 tsp salt

BAGHAAR

2 tbsp ghee

1 onion, sliced

1 tsp mixed mustard and onion seeds

1 Rinse the dals twice under cold running water, removing any stones.

2 Place the dals in a large pan and pour over the water, stirring. Add the ginger, garlic, and red chilies and bring to a boil for 15–20 minutes, over medium heat, half covered with a lid, until soft.

3 Remove the pan from the heat and mash the dals with a potato masher. Add more water if necessary to form a thick sauce.

4 Add the salt to the dal mixture and stir well. Transfer the dal to a heatproof serving dish and keep warm.

COOK'S TIP

This dish makes a very good accompaniment, especially for a dry vegetarian or meat curry. It also freezes well—simply reheat it in a pan or covered in the oven.

2

3

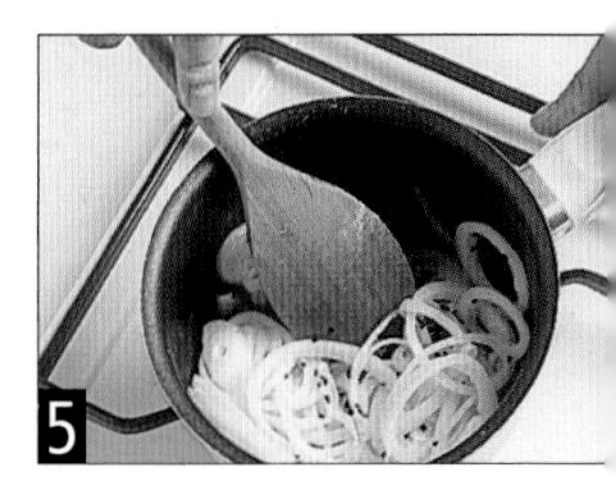
5

5 Just before serving, melt the ghee in a small pan. Add the onion and cook until golden brown. Add the mustard and onion seeds and stir to mix.

6 Pour the onion mixture over the dal while still hot and serve immediately.

spiced rice & lentils

serves four

1 cup basmati rice
¾ cup masoor dal
2 tbsp ghee
1 small onion, sliced
1 tsp chopped fresh gingerroot
1 garlic clove, crushed
½ tsp ground turmeric
2½ cups water
1 tsp salt
Chutney (see pages 223–227), to serve

COOK'S TIP

Many Indian recipes specify ghee as the cooking fat. This is because it is similar to clarified butter in that it can be heated to a very high temperature without burning. Ghee adds a nutty flavor to dishes and a glossy shine to sauces. You can buy ghee in cans, and a vegetarian version is also available. Store at room temperature or keep in the refrigerator.

1 Mix the rice and dal and rinse twice under cold running water, rubbing with your fingers and removing any stones. Reserve.

2 Heat the ghee in a large pan. Add the onion and cook, stirring occasionally, for 2 minutes.

3 Reduce the heat, then add the ginger, garlic, and turmeric and stir-fry for 1 minute.

VARIATION

Moong dal may be substituted for masoor dal in this recipe.

4 Add the rice and dal to the mixture in the pan and blend together, mixing gently.

5 Add the water and bring to a boil Reduce the heat and cook, covered, for 20–25 minutes.

6 Just before serving, add the salt and mix well.

7 Transfer to a serving dish and serve immediately with a Chutney of your choice.

pilaf rice

serves two–four

- 1 cup basmati rice
- 2 tbsp ghee
- 3 green cardamoms
- 2 cloves
- 3 peppercorns
- ½ tsp salt
- ½ tsp saffron threads
- 1¾ cups water

1 Rinse the rice twice under cold running water and reserve.

2 Heat the ghee in a pan. Add the cardamoms, cloves, and peppercorns to the pan and cook, stirring, for 1 minute.

3 Add the rice and stir-fry for an additional 2 minutes.

4 Add the salt, saffron, and water to the rice mixture and reduce the heat. Cover the pan and let simmer over low heat until the water has evaporated.

5 Transfer to a serving dish and serve hot.

COOK'S TIP

The most expensive of all spices, saffron threads are the stamens of a type of crocus. They give dishes a rich, golden color, as well as adding a distinctive, slightly bitter taste. Saffron is sold as a powder or in threads. Saffron threads are more expensive, but do have a superior flavor. Some books recommend substituting ground turmeric—but though the colors are similar, the tastes are not.

tomato rice with bell pepper

serves four

2 cups basmati rice
2 tbsp ghee or vegetable oil
¼ tsp onion seeds
¼ tsp black onion seeds
1 onion, thinly sliced
1 yellow bell pepper, seeded and sliced
4 tomatoes, sliced
1 potato, diced
1 tsp Garlic Paste (see page 7)
1 tsp Ginger Paste (see page 7)
1 tsp chili powder
½ cup frozen fava beans or peas
1 tbsp chopped cilantro
salt
3 cups water
cilantro sprigs, to garnish

1 Rinse the rice in several changes of water and let soak for 10 minutes.

2 Meanwhile, heat the ghee in a large, heavy-bottom pan. Add the onion and black onion seeds and cook over low heat, stirring, for 1–2 minutes, or until they give off their aroma. Add the onion and cook, stirring occasionally, for 5 minutes, or until softened. Drain the rice.

3 Add the yellow bell pepper, tomatoes, potato, Garlic Paste, Ginger Paste, and chili powder and cook, stirring constantly, for 3 minutes. Add the fava beans and cilantro and add salt to taste, then cook, stirring, for 2 minutes.

4 Add the rice and stir until the grains glisten and the ingredients are thoroughly blended. Pour in the water and bring to a boil over high heat. Cover tightly, then reduce the heat and let simmer for 15 minutes.

5 Remove the pan from the heat and let stand, still covered, for 5 minutes. Serve garnished with cilantro sprigs.

COOK'S TIP

The word "basmati" means fragrant in Hindi, and this type of rice is very aromatic. However, you can use other varieties of long-grain rice for this dish, if you prefer.

3

3

4

brown rice with fruit & nuts

serves four–six

4 tbsp ghee or vegetable oil
1 large onion, chopped
2 garlic cloves, crushed
1-inch/2.5-cm piece fresh gingerroot, finely chopped
1 tsp chili powder
1 tsp cumin seeds
1 tbsp mild or medium curry powder or paste
scant 1½ cups brown rice
3¾ cups boiling vegetable stock
2 cups canned chopped tomatoes
salt and pepper
1 cup no-soak dried apricots or peaches, cut into slivers
1 red bell pepper, seeded and diced
¾ cup frozen peas
1–2 small, slightly green bananas
⅓–½ cup toasted mixed nuts

1 Heat the ghee in a large skillet. Add the onion and cook gently for 3 minutes.

2 Stir in the garlic, ginger, chili powder, cumin seeds, curry powder, and rice. Cook gently for 2 minutes, stirring constantly, until the rice is coated in the spiced oil.

2

3 Pour in the boiling stock, stirring to mix. Add the tomatoes and season to taste with salt and pepper. Bring the mixture to a boil, then reduce the heat and let simmer gently, covered, for 40 minutes, or until the rice is almost cooked and most of the liquid is absorbed.

3

3

4 Add the apricots, red bell pepper, and peas to the rice mixture in the skillet. Cover and continue cooking for 10 minutes.

5 Remove the skillet from the heat and let stand for 5 minutes without uncovering.

6 Peel and slice the bananas. Uncover the rice mixture and toss with a fork to mix. Add the toasted nuts and sliced banana and toss lightly.

7 Transfer the brown rice, fruit, and nuts to a serving dish and serve.

lamb biryani

serves six

- ⅔ cup milk
- 1 tsp saffron threads
- 5 tbsp ghee
- 3 onions, sliced
- 2 lb 4 oz/1 kg lean cubed lamb
- 7 tbsp plain yogurt
- 1½ tsp finely chopped fresh gingerroot
- 1–2 garlic cloves, crushed
- 2 tsp Garam Masala (see page 7)
- 2 tsp salt
- ¼ tsp ground turmeric
- 2½ cups water
- 2¼ cups basmati rice
- 2 tsp black cumin seeds
- 3 cardamoms
- 4 tbsp lemon juice
- 2 fresh green chilies
- ¼ bunch of cilantro, chopped

1 Boil the milk in a pan with the saffron and reserve. Heat the ghee in a pan. Add the onions and cook until golden. Remove half of the onions and ghee from the pan and place in a bowl.

2 Mix the meat, yogurt, ginger, garlic, Garam Masala, 1 teaspoon of the salt, and turmeric together in a large bowl.

3 Return the pan with the ghee and onions to the heat. Add the meat mixture and stir for 3 minutes, then add the water. Cook over low heat for 45 minutes, stirring occasionally. Check to see whether the meat is tender: if not, add ⅔ cup water and cook for an additional 15 minutes. Once all the water has evaporated, stir-fry for 2 minutes, then reserve.

4 Meanwhile, place the rice in a pan. Add the cumin seeds, cardamoms, remaining salt, and enough water for cooking, and cook over medium heat until the rice is half cooked. Drain. Remove half of the rice and place in a bowl.

5 Spoon the meat mixture on top of the rice in the pan. Add half each of the saffron milk, lemon juice, chilies, and cilantro. Add the reserved onions and ghee, and the other half of the rice, saffron milk, lemon juice, chilies, and cilantro. Cover and cook over low heat for 15–20 minutes, or until the rice is cooked. Stir well and serve hot.

VARIATION

Substitute the lamb with chicken, if you prefer.

1

2

4

shrimp pilaf

serves four

1 lb/450 g frozen shrimp
⅔ cup milk
½ tsp saffron threads
1 tsp chili powder
1 tsp caraway seeds
2 cinnamon sticks
2 green cardamoms
2 onions, sliced
2 bay leaves
1 tsp finely chopped fresh gingerroot
1 tsp salt
2¼ cups basmati rice
5 tbsp ghee
4 tbsp lemon juice
½ bunch of fresh mint leaves

1 Thaw the frozen shrimp by placing them in a bowl of cold water for 2 hours.

2 Boil the milk in a pan and add the saffron. Reserve until required.

3 Place the chili powder, caraway seeds, cinnamon sticks, green cardamoms, half the onion, the bay leaves, ginger, and salt in a mortar and, using a pestle, grind to a fine paste. Reserve.

4 Place the rice in a pan of boiling water and when the rice is half cooked, remove the pan from the heat, drain, and reserve.

5 Heat the ghee in a pan. Add the remaining onion and cook until golden brown. Transfer to a bowl and mix with the lemon juice and mint.

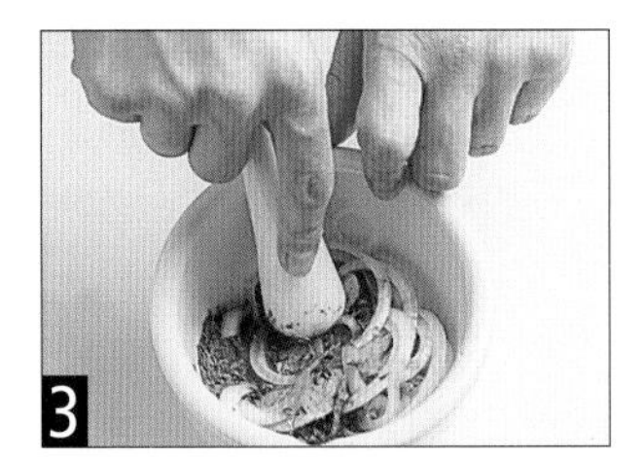
3

6 Add the spice paste and shrimp to the pan and stir-fry for 5 minutes. Remove the shrimp and spices with a slotted spoon and place in a bowl.

7 Place the half-cooked rice in the pan and pour the shrimp mixture over the top. Pour half of the lemon juice, onion and mint mixture, and half of the saffron milk over the shrimp. Arrange the other half of the rice on top and pour over the remaining ingredients.

8 Cover and cook over low heat for 15–20 minutes. Mix well before transferring to a serving dish.

5

6

chicken biryani

serves six

1½ tsp finely chopped fresh gingerroot
1–2 garlic cloves, crushed
1 tbsp Garam Masala (see page 7)
1 tsp chili powder
½ tsp ground turmeric
20 cardamom seeds, crushed
1¼ cups plain yogurt
2 tsp salt
3 lb 5 oz/1.5 kg chicken, skinned and cut into bite-size pieces
⅔ cup milk
pinch of saffron threads
6 tbsp ghee
2 onions, sliced
2¼ cups basmati rice
2 cinnamon sticks
4 black peppercorns
1 tsp black cumin seeds
4 fresh green chilies
½ bunch of cilantro, finely chopped
4 tbsp lemon juice

1 Mix the ginger, garlic, Garam Masala, chili powder, turmeric, cardamom seeds, the yogurt, and 1 teaspoon of the salt together in a bowl. Add the chicken pieces and mix well. Let chill for 3 hours.

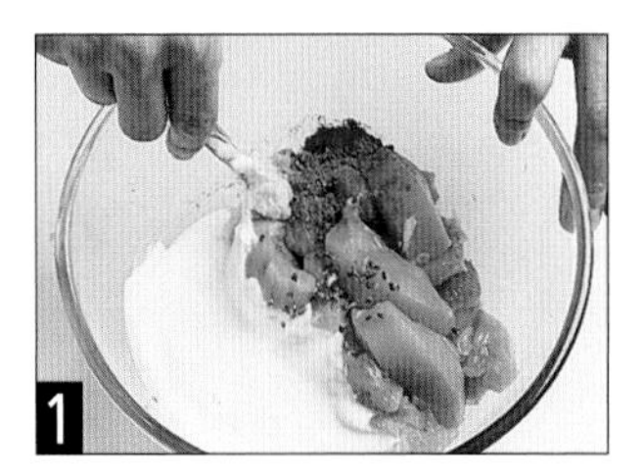

2 Boil the milk in a pan. Place the saffron in a bowl, then pour over the boiling milk. Reserve.

3 Heat the ghee in a large, heavy-bottom pan and cook the onions until golden brown. Remove half of the onions and ghee from the pan and reserve.

4 Place the rice, cinnamon sticks, peppercorns, and cumin seeds in a pan of water. Bring the rice to a boil, then remove the pan from the heat when half cooked. Drain and place in a bowl. Stir in the remaining teaspoon of salt.

5 Chop the chilies. Add the chicken to the pan containing the onions. Add half each of the chilies, cilantro, lemon juice, and saffron milk. Add the rice, then the remaining ingredients, including the fried onions. Cover and cook over low heat for 1 hour. Check that the chicken is well cooked before serving.

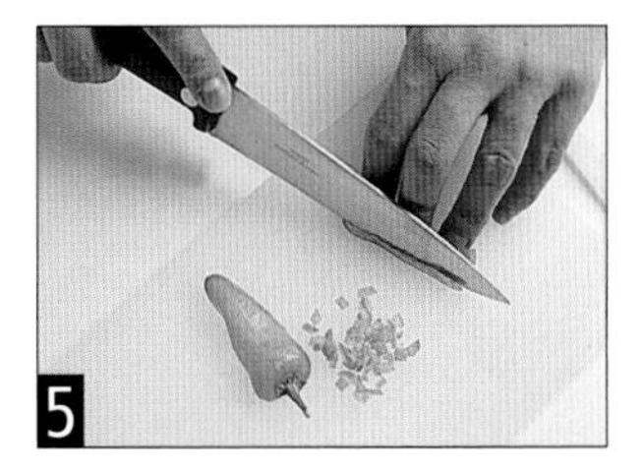

vegetable pilaf

serves four–six

2 potatoes
1 eggplant
7 oz/200 g carrots
⅓ cup green beans
4 tbsp ghee
2 onions, sliced
¾ cup plain yogurt
2 tsp finely chopped fresh gingerroot
2 garlic cloves, crushed
2 tsp Garam Masala (see page 7)
2 tsp black cumin seeds
½ tsp ground turmeric
3 black cardamoms
2 cinnamon sticks
2 tsp salt
1 tsp chili powder
1¼ cups milk
½ tsp saffron threads
3 cups basmati rice
5 tbsp lemon juice

1 Peel and cut the potatoes into 6 pieces. Cut the eggplant into 6 pieces, then peel and slice the carrots and cut the green beans into pieces. Heat the ghee in a skillet. Add the potatoes, eggplant, carrots, and beans, turning with a spatula. Remove from the skillet and reserve.

2 Add the onions to the skillet and cook until soft. Add the yogurt, ginger, garlic, Garam Masala, 1 teaspoon of the cumin seeds, turmeric, 1 cardamom, 1 cinnamon stick, 1 teaspoon of the salt, and the chili powder and stir-fry for 3–5 minutes. Return the vegetables to the skillet and cook for 4–5 minutes.

3 Boil the milk in a pan and add the saffron. Half cook the rice with the remaining salt, cinnamon stick, cardamoms, and cumin seeds in a separate pan of boiling water. Drain the rice, leaving half in the pan while transferring the other half to a bowl.

4 Pour the vegetable mixture on top of the rice in the pan. Pour half of the lemon juice and half of the saffron milk over the vegetables and rice, then cover with the remaining rice and pour the remaining lemon juice and saffron milk over the top. Cover and return to the heat. Cook over low heat for 20 minutes. Serve hot.

1

1

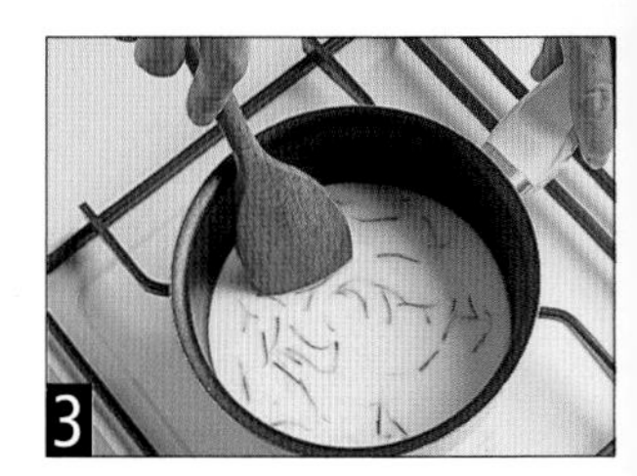
3

tomato rice

serves four

⅔ cup vegetable oil
2 onions, sliced
1 tsp onion seeds
1 tsp finely chopped fresh gingerroot
1 garlic clove, crushed
½ tsp ground turmeric
1 tsp chili powder
1½ tsp salt
2 cups canned tomatoes
2¼ cups basmati rice
2½ cups water

1 Heat the oil in a large pan. Add the onions and cook until golden brown.

2 Add the onion seeds, ginger, garlic, turmeric, chili powder, and salt, stirring well.

3 Reduce the heat, then add the tomatoes and stir-fry for 10 minutes, breaking up the tomatoes.

4 Add the rice to the tomato mixture, stirring gently to coat the rice in the mixture.

5 Pour in the water, stirring to incorporate. Cover the pan and cook over low heat until the water has been absorbed and the rice is cooked.

6 Transfer the tomato rice to a warmed serving dish and serve immediately.

COOK'S TIP

Onion seeds are always used whole in Indian cooking. They are often used in pickles sprinkled over the top of Naan Bread (see page 177). Ironically, onion seeds don't have anything to do with the vegetable, but they look similar to the plant's seed, hence the name.

naan bread

serves six–eight

1 tsp sugar

1 tsp fresh yeast

⅔ warm water

1⅓ cups all-purpose flour, plus extra for dusting

1 tbsp ghee

1 tsp salt

scant ¼ cup unsalted butter, melted

1 tsp poppy seeds

1 Place the sugar and yeast in a small bowl or pitcher with the warm water and mix well until the yeast has dissolved. Let stand for 10 minutes, until the mixture is frothy.

2 Place the flour in a large bowl. Make a well in the center and add the ghee and salt. Pour in the yeast mixture and, using your hands, mix well to form a dough. Add more water if required.

3 Turn the dough out onto a floured counter and knead for 5 minutes, or until smooth.

4 Return the dough to the bowl, then cover and let rise in a warm place for 1½ hours, or until it has doubled in size.

5 Preheat the broiler to very hot. Turn the dough out onto a floured counter and knead for an additional 2 minutes. Break off small balls with your hands and pat them into circles about 5 inches/13 cm in diameter and ½ inch/1 cm thick.

6 Place the dough circles onto a greased sheet of foil and cook under the hot broiler for 7–10 minutes, turning twice and brushing with the butter and sprinkling with the poppy seeds.

7 Serve warm immediately, or keep wrapped in foil until required.

COOK'S TIP

A tandoor oven throws out a ferocious heat; this bread is traditionally cooked on the side wall of the oven where the heat is only slightly less than in the center. For an authentic effect, leave your broiler on for a long time to heat up before the first dough round goes under.

parathas

makes twelve

generous 2 cups whole-wheat flour (urid dal flour [ata] or chapati flour), plus extra for dusting

⅓ cup all-purpose flour

salt

2 tbsp ghee, melted

COOK'S TIP

Press each paratha down gently with a spatula or flat spoon while you are cooking it to make sure that it cooks evenly on both sides.

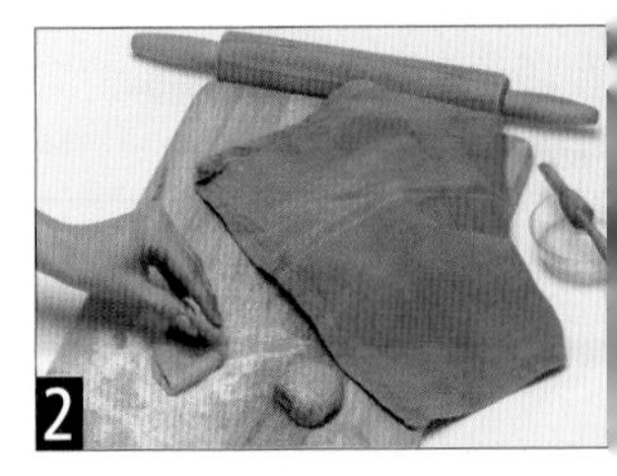

1 Sift the whole-wheat flour, all-purpose flour, and a pinch of salt into a large bowl. Make a well in the center of the flours and add 2 teaspoons of the ghee. Rub it into the flour with your fingertips, then gradually knead in enough cold water to make a soft dough. Cover with plastic wrap and let rest for at least 30 minutes.

2 Divide the dough into 12 equal-size pieces and roll into balls. Keep covered the balls that you are not working on, to prevent them drying out. Roll out a ball of dough on a lightly floured counter to a 4-inch/10-cm circle and brush with ghee. Fold in half, then brush with ghee again and fold in half once more. Either shape into a ball and roll out to a 7-inch/18-cm round or roll into a 6-inch/15-cm triangle. Repeat with the remaining balls, stacking the parathas interleaved with plastic wrap.

3 Heat a heavy-bottom skillet or griddle pan. Add 1–2 parathas at a time and cook for 1 minute, then flip over with a spatula and cook for an additional 2 minutes. Brush with ghee and flip back to the first side and cook until golden. Brush with ghee, then flip over again and cook until golden. Keep warm while you cook the remaining parathas in the same way.

parathas stuffed with vegetables

serves four–six

DOUGH

generous 1⅓ cups whole-wheat flour (urid dal flour [ata] or chapati flour)

½ tsp salt

generous ¾ cup water

scant ½ cup ghee, plus extra for rolling out and frying

FILLING

3 potatoes, peeled and cut into pieces

½ tsp ground turmeric

1 tsp Garam Masala (see page 7)

1 tsp finely chopped fresh gingerroot

¼ bunch of cilantro, chopped

3 fresh green chilies, finely chopped

1 tsp salt

1 To make the parathas, mix the flour, salt, water, and ghee together in a bowl to form a dough.

1

2

2 Divide the dough into 8–12 equal portions. Roll each portion out onto a floured counter. Brush the center of the dough portions with ½ teaspoon of ghee. Fold the dough portions in half, then roll into a pipelike shape and flatten with the palms of your hand, then roll around your finger to form a coil. Roll out again, using flour to dust as and when necessary, to form a circle 7 inches/18 cm in diameter.

3 To make the filling, place the potatoes in a pan of water and cook until soft enough to be mashed. Remove the pan from the heat and mash the potatoes with a potato masher.

4 Blend the turmeric, Garam Masala, ginger, cilantro, chilies, and salt together in a bowl.

5

5 Add the spice mixture to the mashed potato and mix well. Spread 1 tablespoon of the spicy potato mixture on half the dough round and cover with another dough round. Seal the edges well.

6 Heat 2 teaspoons of the ghee in a heavy-bottom skillet. Place the parathas gently in the skillet in batches and cook, turning and moving them about gently with a flat spoon, until golden.

7 Remove the parathas from the skillet and serve immediately.

lightly fried bread

serves five

generous 1⅓ cups whole-wheat flour (urid dal flour (ata) or chapati flour), plus extra for dusting

½ tsp salt

1 tbsp ghee, plus extra for frying

1¼ cups water

COOK'S TIP

In India, breads are cooked on a tava, a traditional flat griddle. A large skillet makes an adequate substitute.

1 Place the whole-wheat flour and the salt in a large bowl and mix well.

2 Make a well in the center of the flour. Add the ghee and rub it in well. Gradually pour in the water and work to form a soft dough. Let the dough rest for 10–15 minutes.

3 Carefully knead the dough for 5–7 minutes. Divide the dough into about 10 equal-size portions.

4 Roll out each dough portion on a lightly floured counter to form a flat crêpe shape.

5 Using a sharp knife, lightly draw lines in a criss cross pattern on each dough portion.

6 Heat a heavy-bottom skillet. Gently place the dough portions, one by one, into the skillet.

7 Cook the bread for 1 minute, then turn over and spread with 1 teaspoon of ghee. Turn the bread over again and cook gently, moving it around the skillet with a spatula, until golden. Turn the bread over once again, then remove from the skillet and keep warm while you cook the remaining batches.

2

4

7

gram flour bread

serves four–six

scant ⅔ cup whole-wheat flour (urid dal flour [ata] or chapati flour), plus extra for dusting
½ cup besan (gram flour)
½ tsp salt
1 small onion
¼ bunch of cilantro, very finely chopped
2 fresh green chilies, finely chopped
⅔ cup water
2 tsp ghee

1 Sift the whole-wheat and gram flours together in a large bowl. Add the salt to the flour and mix well.

2 Finely chop the onion and add to the flour mixture with the cilantro and chilies. Mix well.

3 Add the water and mix to form a soft dough. Cover the dough and let stand for 15 minutes.

4 Knead the dough for 5–7 minutes.

5 Divide the dough into 8 equal-size portions.

6 Roll out the dough portions on a lightly floured counter to circles about 7 inches/18 cm in diameter.

7 Place the dough portions individually in a skillet and cook over medium heat, turning 3 times and lightly greasing each side with the ghee each time.Transfer the bread to serving plates and serve hot.

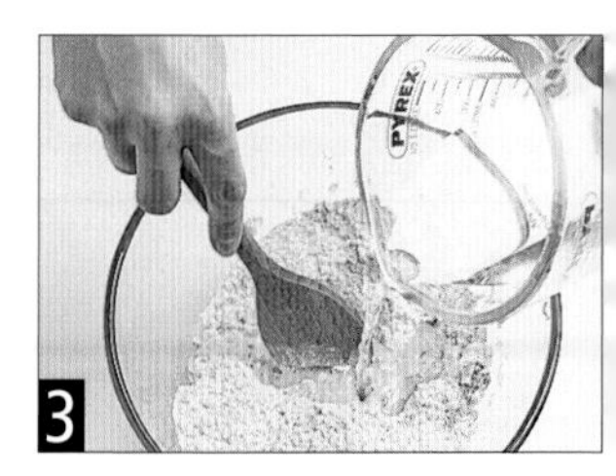

COOK'S TIP

Also called gram flour, besan is a pale yellow flour made from ground chickpeas. In Indian kitchens it is used to make breads, bhajias, and batters and to thicken sauces and stabilize yogurt when it is added to hot dishes. Buy it from Indian groceries or large health food stores and store in a cool, dark place in an airtight container.

pooris

serves ten

generous 1⅓ cups whole-wheat flour (urid dal flour (ata) or chapati flour)

½ tsp salt

⅔ cup water

2½ cups vegetable oil, plus extra for oiling

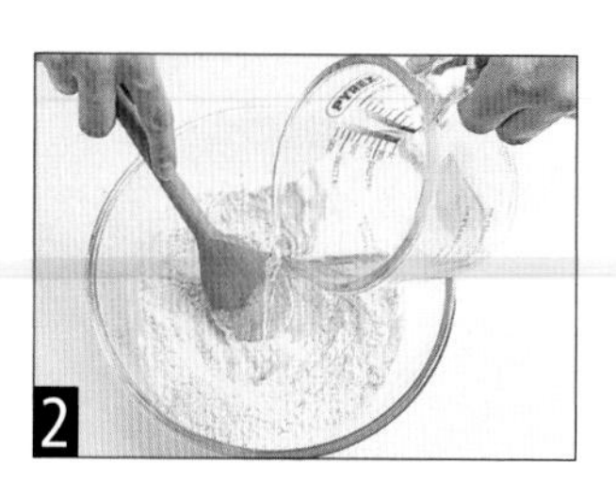

2

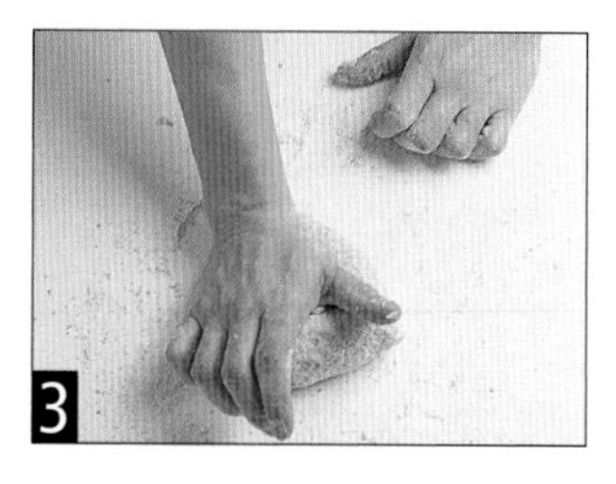

3

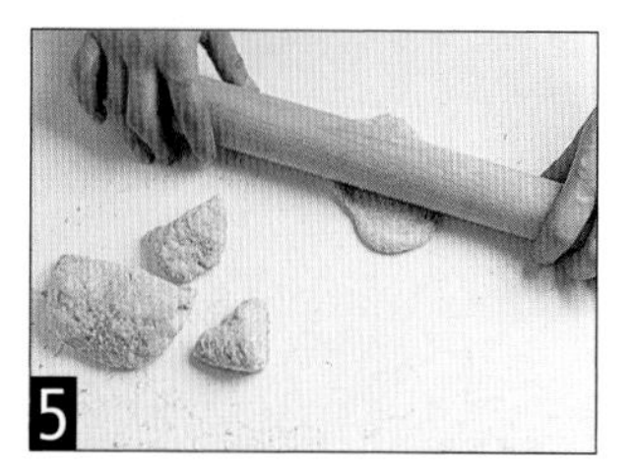

5

1 Place the flour and salt in a large bowl and stir well.

2 Make a well in the center of the flour. Gradually pour in the water and mix together to form a dough, adding more water if necessary.

3 Knead the dough until it is smooth and elastic and let rest in a warm place for 15 minutes.

4 Divide the dough into 10 equal portions and with lightly oiled hands, pat each into a smooth ball.

5 Roll out each ball on a lightly oiled counter to form a thin circle.

6 Heat the oil in a deep skillet. Deep-fry the circles in batches for a few seconds, turning once, until golden in color.

7 Remove the pooris and drain on paper towels. Serve hot.

COOK'S TIP

You can make pooris in advance, if you prefer. Wrap in foil and reheat in a hot oven for 10 minutes when required.

chapatis

serves five–six

generous 1⅓ cups whole-wheat flour (urid dal flour [ata] or chapati flour), plus extra for dusting
½ tsp salt
generous ¾ cup water

1 Place the flour in a large bowl. Add the salt and mix well.

2 Make a well in the center of the flour and gradually pour in the water, mixing well with your fingers to form a supple dough.

3 Knead the dough for 7–10 minutes. Ideally, let the dough rest for 15–20 minutes, but if time is short roll out the dough straightaway. Divide the dough into 10–12 equal-size portions. Roll out each piece of dough on a well floured counter.

COOK'S TIP

Ideally, chapatis should be eaten as they come out of the skillet, but if that is not practical keep them warm after cooking by wrapping them up in foil. In India, chapatis are sometimes cooked on a naked flame, which makes them puff up. Allow about 2 per person.

4 Place a heavy-bottom skillet on a high heat. When steam begins to rise from the skillet, reduce the heat to medium.

5 Place a chapati in the skillet and when the chapati begins to bubble turn it over. Carefully press down on the chapati with a clean dish towel or a wooden spatula and turn the chapati over once again. Remove the chapati from the skillet and keep warm while you make the others.

6 Repeat the process until all of the chapatis are cooked.

Snacks & Side Dishes

In India, people enjoy holding tea parties at about 5 or 6 o'clock in the afternoon, and little snacks such as the ones in this chapter are served. They are ideal for cocktail or other drinks parties, when you would like to offer something more interesting than the usual peanuts and chips. The basic quantities are for 4 people, but you can multiply according to the number on your guest list. Accompaniments—a simple Cucumber Salad (see page 210) or a Mint Raita (see page 222), for example—always add color and variety to a meal. Most take very little time to prepare, but taste delicious. None of these accompaniments has to be made in large quantities, because they are taken in only small amounts: variety is better than quantity!

onion bhajias

makes about twenty-four

- ½ tsp onion seeds
- ½ tsp cumin seeds
- ½ tsp fennel seeds
- ½ tsp black onion seeds
- generous 1½ cups besan
- 1 tsp baking powder
- 1 tsp ground turmeric
- ½ tsp chili powder
- pinch of asafetida
- salt
- 3 onions, thinly sliced
- 2 fresh green chilies, seeded and finely chopped
- 3 tbsp chopped cilantro
- vegetable oil, for deep-frying

COOK'S TIP

Do not overcrowd the fryer or pan when deep-frying, because you need room to turn the bhajias over. Lower the bhajias slowly into the hot oil to prevent any splashes.

1 Heat a large, heavy-bottom skillet and dry-fry the onion, cumin, fennel, and black onion seeds for a few seconds, stirring constantly, until they give off their aroma. Remove from the heat and tip into a mortar. Crush lightly with a pestle and tip into a large bowl.

2 Sift the besan, baking powder, turmeric, chili powder, asafetida, and a pinch of salt into the bowl and add the onions, chilies, and chopped cilantro. Mix thoroughly, then gradually stir in enough cold water to make a thick batter.

3 Heat the oil in a deep-fat fryer or large, heavy-bottom pan to 350–375°F/180–190°C, or until a cube of bread browns in 30 seconds. Drop spoonfuls of the mixture into the hot oil and cook until golden brown, turning once. Remove with a slotted spoon and drain on paper towels. Serve hot.

VARIATION

You can use this batter to make bhajias with a variety of other vegetables, such as cauliflower florets or sliced mushrooms.

pakoras

serves four

- 6 tbsp besan
- ½ tsp salt
- 1 tsp chili powder
- 1 tsp baking powder
- 1½ tsp white cumin seeds
- 1 tsp pomegranate seeds
- 1¼ cups water
- ¼ bunch of cilantro, finely chopped
- vegetables of your choice: cauliflower, cut into small florets; onions, cut into rings; potatoes, sliced; eggplants, sliced; or fresh spinach leaves
- vegetable oil, for deep-frying

1 Sift the besan into a large bowl.

2 Add the salt, chili powder, baking powder, cumin, and pomegranate seeds and blend together well.

3 Pour in the water and beat well to form a smooth batter.

4 Add the chopped cilantro and mix. Reserve.

5 Dip the prepared vegetables of your choice into the batter, carefully shaking off any excess.

COOK'S TIP

When deep-frying, it is important to use oil at the correct temperature. If the oil is too hot, the outside of the food will burn, as will the spices, before the inside is cooked. If the oil is too cool, the food will be sodden with oil before a crisp batter forms. Draining on paper towels is essential, because it absorbs excess oil and moisture.

6 Heat the oil in a large heavy-bottom skillet. Place the battered vegetables in the oil and deep-fry, in batches, turning once.

7 Repeat this process until all of the batter has been used up.

8 Transfer the battered vegetables to paper towels and drain thoroughly. Serve immediately.

2

3

5

dal fritters

serves four

- ½ cup moong dal, soaked for 2–3 hours, then drained
- ½ cup urid dal, soaked for 2–3 hours, then drained
- 1–2 tbsp water
- 1 onion, finely chopped
- 1 fresh green chili, chopped
- 1-inch/2.5-cm piece fresh gingerroot, finely chopped
- 1 tbsp chopped cilantro
- ¼ tsp baking soda
- salt
- vegetable oil, for deep-frying
- Chutney (see pages 223–227), to serve

1 Place the dals in a food processor with the water and process to make a thick paste. Transfer to a large bowl and stir in the onion, chili, ginger, cilantro, and baking soda. Season with salt to taste, then mix thoroughly and let stand for 5 minutes.

2 Heat the oil in a deep-fat fryer or large, heavy-bottom pan to 350–375°F/180–190°C, or until a cube of bread browns in 30 seconds. Drop small spoonfuls of the mixture into the hot oil and deep-fry for 3–4 minutes, or until golden.

3 Remove the fritters with a slotted spoon and drain on paper towels. Keep warm while you cook the remaining fritters. Serve immediately with the Chutney of your choice.

VARIATION

Substitute ½–1 teaspoon of chili powder for the fresh chili, if you like. Serve with either Mango or Tamarind Chutney (see pages 226–227).

fried eggplants in yogurt

serves four

generous ¾ cup plain yogurt

generous ¼ cup water

1 tsp salt

1 eggplant

⅔ cup vegetable oil

1 tsp white cumin seeds

6 dried red chilies

COOK'S TIP

Rich in protein and calcium, yogurt plays an important part in Indian cooking. It is used as a marinade, as a creamy flavoring in curries and sauces, and as a cooling accompaniment to hot dishes.

VARIATION

Finely chop and seed the dried red chilies, if you prefer.

1 Place the yogurt in a bowl and whisk with a fork. Add the water and salt to the yogurt and mix well.

2 Transfer the yogurt mixture to a serving bowl and reserve.

3 Using a sharp knife, slice the eggplant thinly.

4 Heat the oil in a large skillet. Add the eggplant slices and cook, in batches, over medium heat, turning occasionally, for 5 minutes, until they begin to turn crisp. Remove from the skillet, then transfer to a serving plate and keep warm.

5 When all of the eggplant slices have been cooked, reduce the heat and add the cumin seeds and the dried red chilies to the skillet. Cook for 1 minute, stirring.

6 Spoon the yogurt on top of the eggplants, then pour over the cumin and chilli mixture. Serve immediately.

spicy corn

serves four

- 1¾ cups frozen or canned corn
- 1 tsp ground cumin
- 1 garlic clove, crushed
- 1 tsp ground coriander
- 1 tsp salt
- 2 fresh green chilies, chopped
- 1 onion, finely chopped
- 3 tbsp unsalted butter
- 4 dried red chilies, crushed
- ½ tsp lemon juice
- ¼ bunch of cilantro, shredded, plus extra to garnish

1 Thaw the corn (or drain if using canned corn) and reserve.

2 Place the ground cumin, garlic, ground coriander, salt, half of the green chili, and the onion in a mortar or a food processor and grind to form a smooth paste.

3 Heat the butter in a large skillet. Add the onion and spice mixture and cook over medium heat, stirring occasionally, for 5–7 minutes.

4 Add the crushed red chilies to the skillet and stir to mix.

5 Add the corn and stir-fry for an additional 2 minutes.

COOK'S TIP

Cilantro is an essential ingredient in Indian cooking, along with coriander seeds from the same plant. Coriander seeds are often dry-roasted before use to develop their flavor.

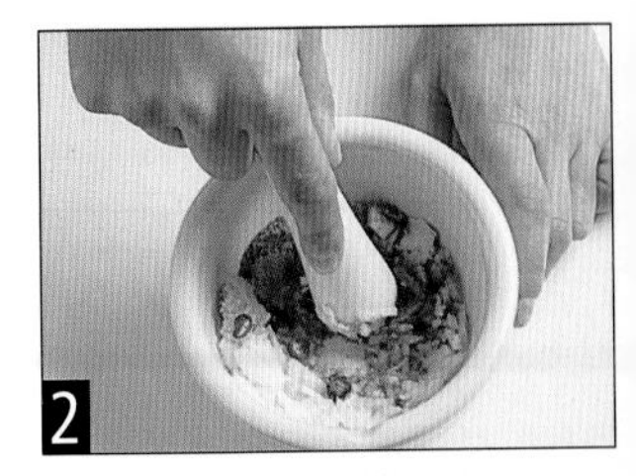

6 Add the remaining green chili, lemon juice, and the shredded cilantro to the skillet, stirring occasionally to mix.

7 Transfer the spicy corn mixture to a warmed serving dish. Garnish with cilantro and serve hot.

indian-style omelet

serves two–four

1 small onion, very finely chopped

2 fresh green chilies, finely chopped

¼ bunch of cilantro, finely chopped

4 eggs

1 tsp salt

2 tbsp vegetable oil

cilantro sprigs, to garnish

crisp green salad, to serve

1 Mix the onion, chilies, and cilantro together in a large bowl.

2 Place the eggs in a separate bowl and whisk together. Add the onion mixture and mix together. Add the salt and whisk together well.

3 Heat 1 tablespoon of the oil in a skillet. Place a ladleful of the omelet mixture into the skillet.

4 Cook the omelet, turning once and pressing down with a wooden spatula to make sure that the egg is cooked right through, until the omelet is golden brown.

5 Repeat the same process with the remaining omelet mixture. Keep the cooked omelets warm in the meantime.

6 Garnish with cilantro sprigs and serve the omelets immediately with a crisp green salad.

COOK'S TIP

Indian cooks use a variety of vegetable oils, and peanut or corn oils make good alternatives for most dishes, although sometimes more specialty ones, such as coconut oil, mustard oil, and sesame oil, are called for.

shrimp patties

makes eight

- 10 oz/280 g cooked shrimp, peeled, deveined, and chopped
- 1 onion, finely chopped
- 1 fresh green chili, seeded and finely chopped
- ½-inch/1-cm piece fresh gingerroot, finely chopped
- 1 tbsp chopped cilantro
- 2 tbsp fresh white bread crumbs
- ¼ tsp ground turmeric
- 1 tbsp lime juice
- 1 egg, lightly beaten
- ⅔ cup dried bread crumbs
- 3 tbsp ghee or vegetable oil
- cilantro sprigs, to garnish

VARIATION

To make chicken patties, substitute the same quantity of ground cooked chicken for the shrimp.

1 Mix the shrimp, onion, chili, ginger, cilantro, fresh bread crumbs, turmeric, lime juice, and beaten egg in a large bowl, kneading well with your hands until the mixture is thoroughly blended.

2 Divide the mixture into 8 equal-size portions, then form each portion into a ball between the palms of your hands and flatten into patties. Spread the dried bread crumbs out on a large plate and dip each patty in turn into the bread crumbs to coat evenly.

3 Heat the ghee in a large, heavy-bottom skillet. Add the patties, in 2 batches if necessary, and cook for 5–6 minutes on each side, until golden brown. Remove with a spatula and drain on paper towels. Keep each batch warm while you cook the remainder. Garnish with cilantro sprigs and serve immediately.

COOK'S TIP

If possible, use natural dried bread crumbs for coating the patties rather than colored bread crumbs. You may need to press the bread crumbs onto the patties to coat.

vegetable sambar

serves six

4 cups canned tomatoes
2 tbsp dry unsweetened coconut
2 tbsp lemon juice
1 tbsp yellow mustard seeds
scant ¼ cup raw or muscovado sugar
2 tbsp ghee or vegetable oil
2 onions, sliced
4 cardamom pods, lightly crushed
6 curry leaves, plus extra to garnish
2 tsp ground coriander
2 tsp ground cumin
1 tsp ground turmeric
1 tsp Ginger Paste (see page 7)
scant 1 cup toor dal
1 lb/450 g sweet potatoes, cut into chunks
2 lb/900 g potatoes, cut into chunks
2 carrots, sliced
2 zucchini, cut into chunks
1 eggplant, cut into chunks
salt

1 Place the tomatoes and their can juices, coconut, 1 tablespoon of the lemon juice, the mustard seeds, and sugar in a food processor or blender and process until smooth.

2 Heat the ghee in a large, heavy-bottom pan. Add the onion and cook over low heat, stirring occasionally, for 10 minutes, or until golden. Add the cardamoms, curry leaves, coriander, cumin, turmeric, and Ginger Paste and cook, stirring constantly, for 1–2 minutes, or until the spices give off their aroma. Stir in the tomato mixture and dal and bring to a boil. Reduce the heat, then cover and simmer for 10 minutes.

3 Add the sweet potatoes, potatoes, and carrots. Re-cover the pan and simmer for an additional 15 minutes. Add the zucchini, eggplant, and remaining lemon juice and salt to taste, then re-cover and simmer for an additional 10–15 minutes, or until the vegetables are tender. Serve garnished with curry leaves.

VARIATION

You can use any vegetables that you have to hand to make this dish. Add fibrous ones with the sweet potatoes and softer ones with the zucchini.

1

2

3

soft dumplings in yogurt with masala

serves four

1⅓ cups urid dal flour (ata)
1 tsp baking powder
½ tsp ground ginger
1¼ cups water
vegetable oil, for deep-frying

YOGURT SAUCE
1¾ cups plain yogurt
⅔ cup water
generous ⅓ cup sugar

MASALA
⅓ cup ground coriander
⅓ cup ground white cumin
1–2 tsp dried chili flakes
3½ oz/100 g citric acid
chopped fresh red chilies, to garnish

1 Place the urid dal flour in a large bowl. Add the baking powder and ground ginger and stir well. Add the water and mix to form a batter.

2 Heat the oil in a deep pan or skillet. Pour in the batter, 1 teaspoon at a time, and deep-fry the dumplings until golden brown, reducing the heat when the oil gets too hot. Set the dumplings aside.

3 To make the yogurt sauce, place the yogurt in a separate bowl. Add the water and sugar and mix together with a whisk or fork. Reserve until required.

1

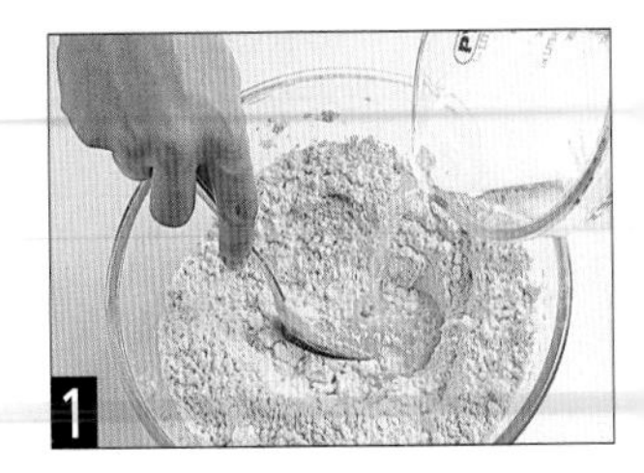
1

4

4 To make the masala, dry-roast the ground coriander and the cumin in a pan until a little darker in color. Add the dried chili flakes and citric acid and blend well together.

5 Sprinkle 1 tablespoon of the masala over the dumplings and garnish with chopped red chilies. Serve with the reserved yogurt mixture.

samosas

serves ten–twelve

PASTRY

⅔ cup self-rising flour

½ tsp salt

3 tbsp butter, cut into small pieces

4 tbsp water

FILLING

3 potatoes, boiled

1 tsp finely chopped fresh gingerroot

1 garlic clove, crushed

½ tsp white cumin seeds

½ tsp mixed onion and mustard seeds

1 tsp salt

½ tsp dried red chili flakes

2 tbsp lemon juice

2 small fresh green chilies, finely chopped

vegetable oil, for deep-frying

1 Sift the flour and salt into a large bowl. Add the butter and rub it into the flour until the mixture resembles fine bread crumbs.

2 Pour in the water and mix with a fork to form a dough. Pat the dough into a ball and knead for 5 minutes, or until the dough is smooth. Add a little flour if the dough is sticky. Cover and reserve.

3 To make the filling, mash the boiled potatoes gently and mix with the ginger, garlic, cumin seeds, onion and mustard seeds, salt, dried red chili flakes, lemon juice, and green chili.

4 Break small balls off the dough and roll each one out very thinly to form a round. Cut in half, then dampen the edges and shape into cones. Fill the cones with a little of the filling, then dampen the top and bottom edges of the cones and pinch together to seal. Reserve.

5 Fill a deep pan one-third full with oil and heat to 350°–375°F/180°–190°C, or until a small cube of bread browns in 30 seconds. Lower the samosas into the oil, a few at a time, and deep-fry for 2–3 minutes or until golden brown. Remove from the oil and drain thoroughly on paper towels. Serve hot or cold.

samosas with meat filling

serves ten–twelve

1 quantity Samosa Pastry (see page 201)

vegetable oil, for deep-frying

cilantro sprigs, to garnish

FILLING

2 tbsp ghee or vegetable oil

1 onion, chopped

1 lb/450 g fresh ground lamb

1 tsp Garlic Paste (see page 7)

1 tsp Ginger Paste (see page 7)

salt and pepper

COOK'S TIP

Frozen samosas do not need to be thawed before deep-frying. However, if you prefer to thaw them, this will not adversely affect them.

1 To make the filling, heat the ghee in a karahi or large, heavy-bottom skillet. Add the onion and cook over low heat, stirring frequently, for 10 minutes, or until golden. Add the lamb, Garlic Paste, and Ginger Paste and season to taste with salt and pepper. Cook, breaking up the meat with a wooden spoon, for 10 minutes, or until the mixture is fairly dry. Transfer to a bowl with a slotted spoon and let cool.

2 Break small balls off the dough and roll each one out very thinly to form a circle. Cut in half, then dampen the edges and form into cones. Fill the cones with some of the filling, then dampen the top and bottom edges and pinch together to seal. Reserve.

3 Fill a deep-fat fryer or large, heavy-bottom pan one-third full with vegetable oil and heat to 350–375°F/180–190°C, or until a cube of bread browns in 30 seconds. Carefully lower the samosas into the hot oil, in batches, and deep-fry for 2–3 minutes, or until golden brown. Remove with a slotted spoon and drain on paper towels. Keep warm while you cook the remaining samosas. Serve hot or cold, garnished with cilantro sprigs.

VARIATION

If you don't want to go to the bother of making the samosa pastry yourself, you can use spring roll wrappers instead.

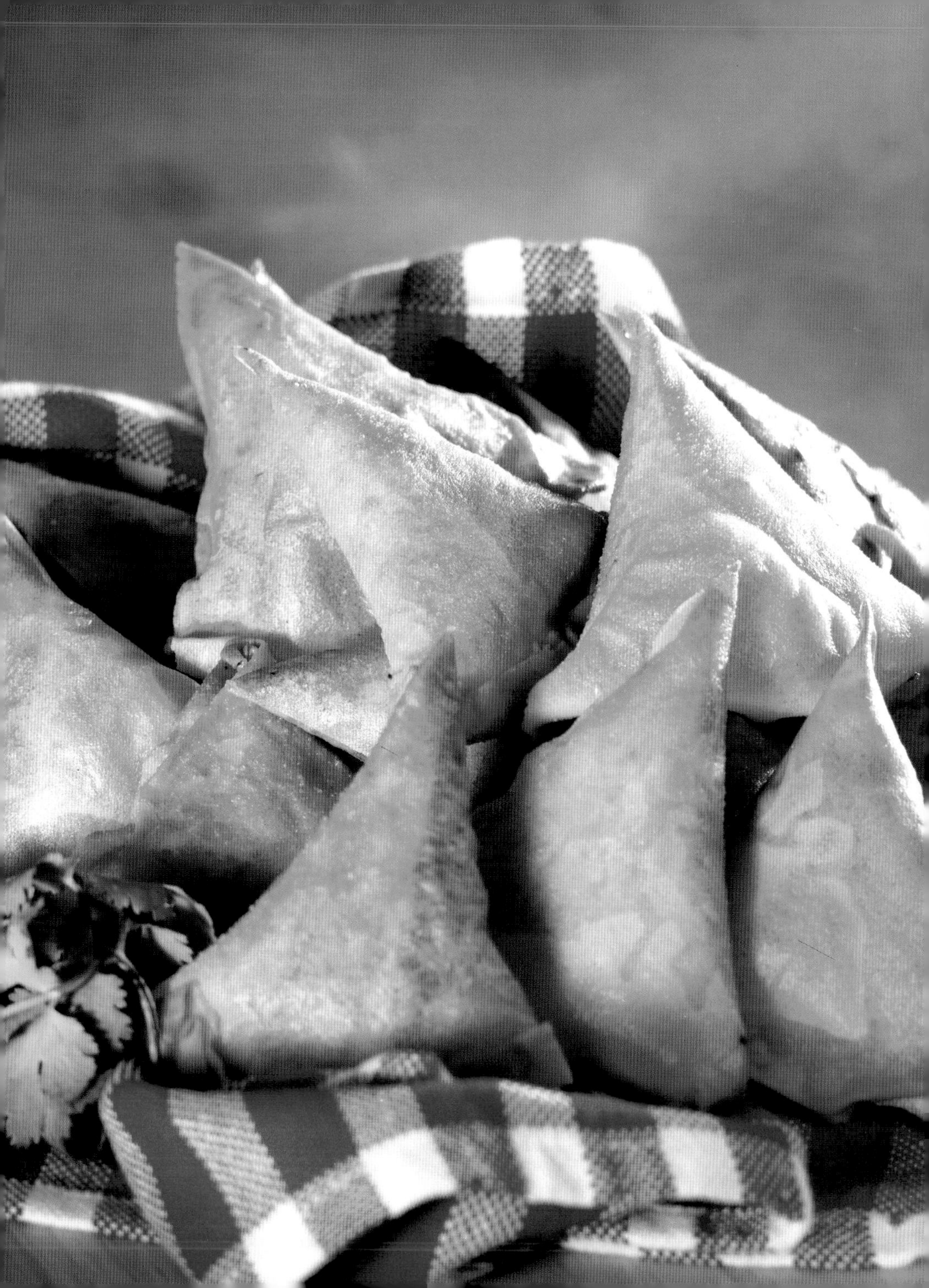

bombay potatoes

serves six

1 lb 2 oz/500 g new potatoes, diced
1 tsp ground turmeric
salt
4 tbsp ghee or vegetable oil
6 curry leaves
1 dried red chili
2 fresh green chilies, chopped
½ tsp black onion seeds
1 tsp mixed mustard and
onion seeds
½ tsp cumin seeds
½ tsp fennel seeds
¼ tsp asafetida
2 onions, chopped
5 tbsp chopped cilantro
juice of ½ lime

1 Place the potatoes in a large, heavy-bottom pan and pour in just enough cold water to cover. Add ½ teaspoon of the turmeric and a pinch of salt and bring to a boil. Simmer for 10 minutes, or until tender, then drain and reserve until required.

2 Heat the ghee in a large, heavy-bottom skillet. Add the curry leaves and dried red chili and cook, stirring frequently, for a few minutes, or until the chili is blackened. Add the remaining turmeric, the fresh chilies, the black onion, mustard, onion, cumin, and fennel seeds and the asafetida, onions, and chopped cilantro and cook, stirring constantly, for 5 minutes, or until the onions have softened.

3 Stir in the potatoes and cook over low heat, stirring frequently, for 10 minutes, or until heated through. Squeeze over the lime juice and serve.

COOK'S TIP

Asafetida is thought to aid digestion and combat flatulence. It is best bought as a powder rather than as a resin, although the powder quickly loses its flavor and must be stored in a sealed jar.

spicy potato cakes

makes eight

1 lb/450 g potatoes, diced

1 onion, grated

1 tsp Garam Masala (see page 7)

¼ tsp chili powder (optional)

1 tbsp lemon juice

2 tbsp chopped cilantro

salt

4 tbsp ghee or butter

cilantro sprigs, to garnish

1 Cook the potatoes in a pan of lightly salted boiling water for 10–15 minutes, or until tender, but still firm. Meanwhile, place the grated onion in a clean dish towel and wring well to squeeze out the excess moisture. Transfer the onion to a large bowl and stir in the Garam Masala, chili powder (if using), lemon juice, and chopped cilantro. Season with salt to taste.

2 Drain the potatoes and add to the bowl. Mash coarsely with a fork or potato masher. Divide the mixture into 8 equal-size portions, then form each portion into a ball between the palms of your hands and flatten into a cake.

3 Heat the ghee in a large, heavy-bottom skillet. Add the potato cakes, in batches, if necessary, and cook for 2 minutes on each side, until golden brown and crisp. Remove from the skillet with a spatula and drain on paper towels. Serve warm or cold garnished with cilantro sprigs.

1

2

3

chickpea snack

serves 2–4

1½ cups canned chickpeas, drained
1 onion
2 potatoes
2 tbsp tamarind paste
6 tbsp water
1 tsp chili powder
2 tsp sugar
1 tsp salt
TO GARNISH
1 tomato, cut into fourths
2 fresh green chilies, chopped
2–3 tbsp chopped cilantro

1 Place the drained chickpeas in a large bowl.

2 Chop the onion and reserve. Peel and dice the potatoes. Place the potatoes in a pan of water and boil until cooked through. Drain and reserve until required.

3 Mix the tamarind paste and water together in a small bowl.

4 Add the chili powder, sugar, and 1 teaspoon of salt to the tamarind paste mixture and mix together. Pour the mixture over the chickpeas.

COOK'S TIP

Cream-colored and resembling hazelnuts in appearance, chickpeas have a nutty flavor and slightly crunchy texture. Indian cooks also grind chickpeas to make a flour called besan or gram flour, which is used to make breads, thicken sauces, and to make batters for deep-fried dishes.

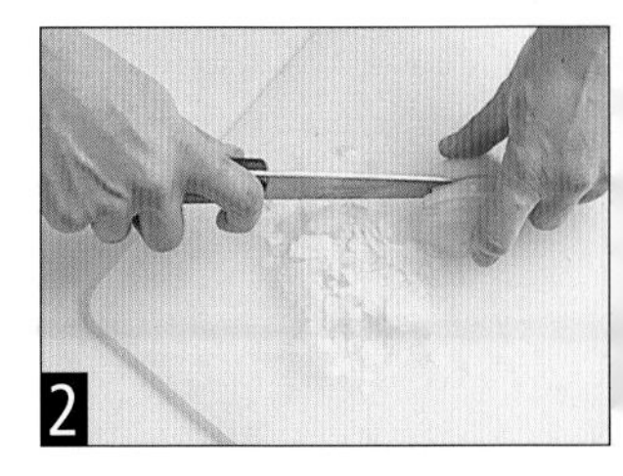
2

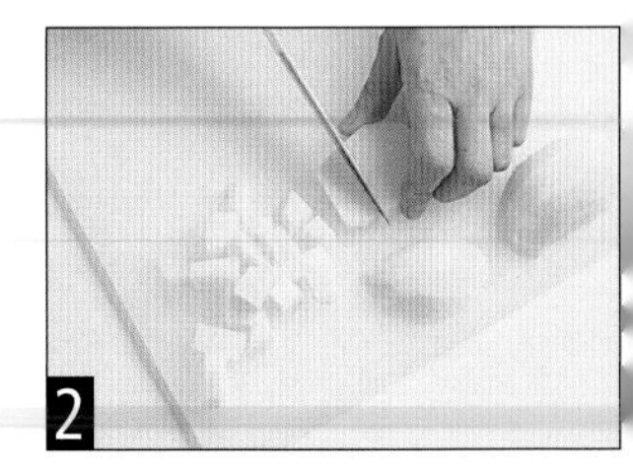
2

3

5 Add the onion and the diced potatoes, and stir to mix. Season with a little salt to taste.

6 Transfer to a serving bowl and garnish with tomato, chilies, and chopped cilantro.

deep-fried diamond pastries

serves four

1 cup all-purpose flour

1 tsp baking powder

½ tsp salt

1 tbsp black cumin seeds

scant ½ cup water

1¼ cups vegetable oil

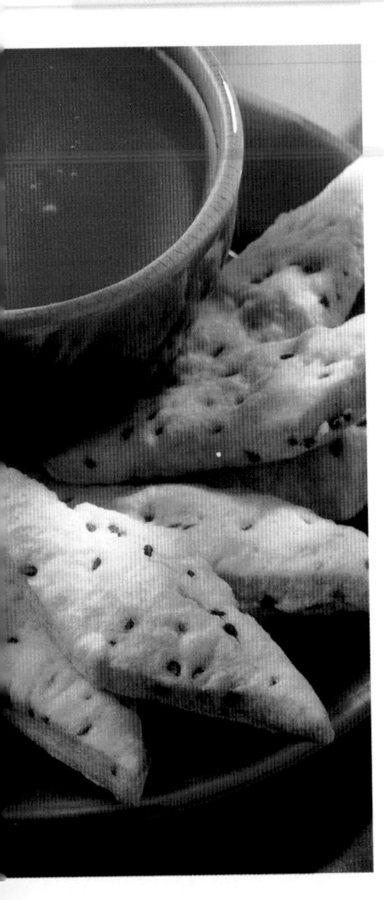

1 Place the all-purpose flour in a large bowl.

2 Add the baking powder, salt, and the cumin seeds and stir to mix.

3 Add the water to the dry ingredients and mix to form a soft, elastic dough.

COOK'S TIP

Black cumin seeds are used here for their strong aromatic flavor. White cumin seeds cannot be used as a substitute.

4 Roll out the dough on a clean counter until ¼ inch/5 mm thick.

5 Using a sharp knife, score the dough to form diamond shapes. Re-roll the dough trimmings and cut out more diamond shapes until all of the dough has been used up.

6 Heat the oil in a large pan to 350°–375°F/180°–190°C, or until a cube of bread browns in 30 seconds.

7 Carefully place the pastry diamonds in the hot oil, in batches if necessary, and deep-fry until golden brown.

8 Remove the diamond pastries with a slotted spoon and let drain on paper towels. Serve with a dal for dipping or store in an airtight container and serve when required.

spiced semolina

serves four

⅔ cup vegetable oil
1 tsp mixed onion and mustard seeds
4 dried red chilies
4 curry leaves (fresh or dried)
8 tbsp coarse semolina
⅓ cup cashew nuts
1 tsp salt
⅔ cup water

COOK'S TIP

Curry leaves are very similar in appearance to bay leaves but are very different in flavor. They can be bought both fresh and dried. They are used to flavor lentil dishes and vegetable curries.

1 Heat the oil in a large, heavy-bottom pan.

2 Add the mixed onion and mustard seeds, dried red chilies, and curry leaves and stir-fry for 1 minute, stirring constantly.

3 Reduce the heat and add the coarse semolina and the cashew nuts to the mixture in the pan. Quickly stir-fry for 5 minutes, moving the mixture around all the time so that it does not catch and burn.

4 Add the salt to the mixture and continue to stir-fry, stirring constantly.

5 Add the water and cook, stirring constantly, until the mixture begins to thicken.

6 Serve the spiced semolina warm as a teatime snack.

cool cucumber salad

serves four

8 oz/225 g cucumber

1 fresh green chili (optional)

2 tbsp finely chopped cilantro

2 tbsp lemon juice

½ tsp salt

1 tsp sugar

fresh mint leaves, to garnish

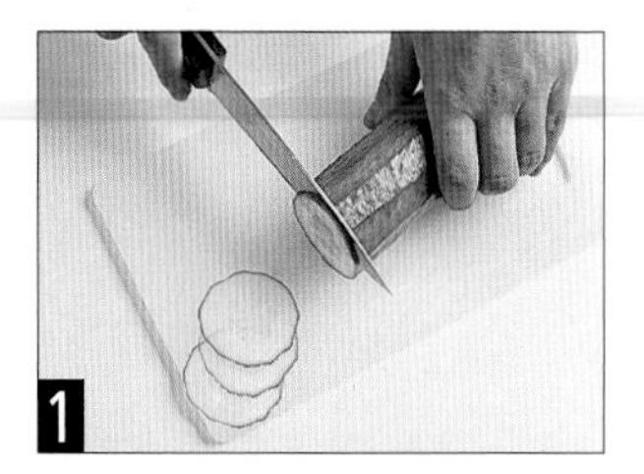

1 Using a sharp knife, slice the cucumber thinly and cut the slices in half. Arrange the cucumber slices on a round serving plate. Using a sharp knife, chop the green chili (if using). Sprinkle the chopped chili over the cucumber.

2 To make the dressing, place the cilantro, lemon juice, salt, and sugar in a bowl and mix together, then reserve.

3 Place the cucumber in the refrigerator and let chill for at least 1 hour, or until required. Transfer the cucumber to a serving dish. Pour the dressing over the cucumber just before serving and garnish with a few mint leaves.

COOK'S TIP

Much of the heat in Indian dishes comes from the use of fresh green chilies, although dried and ground red chilies are also commonplace in Indian kitchens. In southern India, with its searingly hot temperatures, chilies are used in copious amounts because they cause the body to perspire, which has a cooling effect. Numerous varieties of fresh chili grow in India, from fairly mild to hot. As a general rule, the smaller the chili, the hotter it will be. Fresh chilies will keep for about 5 days in the refrigerator. To store cilantro, put the roots in a glass of water and keep in a cool place for up to 4 days.

tomato kachumbar

serves six

- ½ cup lime juice
- ½ tsp sugar
- salt
- 6 tomatoes, chopped
- ½ cucumber, chopped
- 8 scallions, chopped
- 1 fresh green chili, seeded and chopped
- 1 tbsp chopped cilantro
- 1 tbsp chopped fresh mint

1 Mix the lime juice, sugar, and a pinch of salt together in a large bowl and stir until the sugar has completely dissolved.

2 Add the tomatoes, cucumber, scallions, chili, cilantro, and mint and toss well to mix.

3 Cover with plastic wrap and let chill in the refrigerator for at least 30 minutes. Toss the vegetables before serving.

COOK'S TIP

Chop all the vegetables into fairly small, even-size pieces for the best texture and presentation. You can use whatever vegetables you have in the refrigerator, as long as they can be eaten raw.

1

2

3

hot salad

serves four

½ cauliflower

1 green bell pepper

1 red bell pepper

½ cucumber

4 carrots

2 tbsp butter

salt and pepper

COOK'S TIP

In India, you can buy snacks and accompaniments along the roadside. While you can buy many of them from Asian stores, they are fresher and more satisfying made at home.

1 Rinse the cauliflower and cut into small florets, using a sharp knife. Seed and cut the bell peppers into thin strips. Cut the cucumber into thick slices, then into fourths. Peel the carrots and cut them into thin slices.

2 Melt the butter in a large pan, stirring constantly.

3 Add the cauliflower, bell peppers, cucumber, and carrots and stir-fry for 5–7 minutes. Season to taste with salt and pepper. Cover with a lid, then reduce the heat and let simmer for 3 minutes.

4 Transfer the vegetables to a serving dish, toss to mix and serve immediately.

1

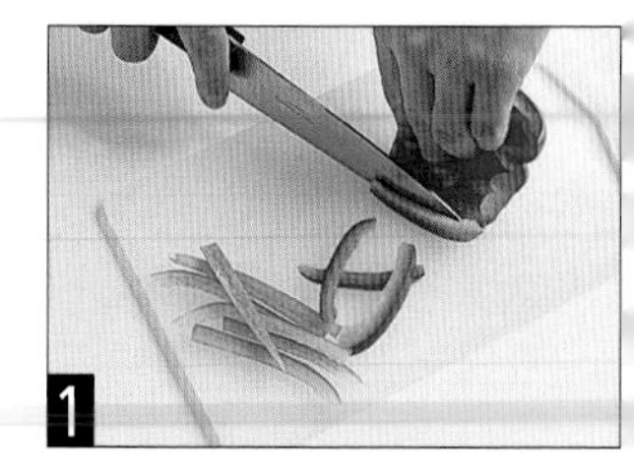

1

3

VARIATION

You can replace the vegetables in this recipe with those of your choice, if you prefer.

sweet & sour fruit

serves four

14 oz/400 g canned mixed fruit cocktail

14 oz/400 g canned guavas

2 large bananas

3 apples

1 tsp coarsely ground pepper

1 tsp salt

2 tbsp lemon juice

½ tsp ground ginger

fresh mint leaves, to garnish

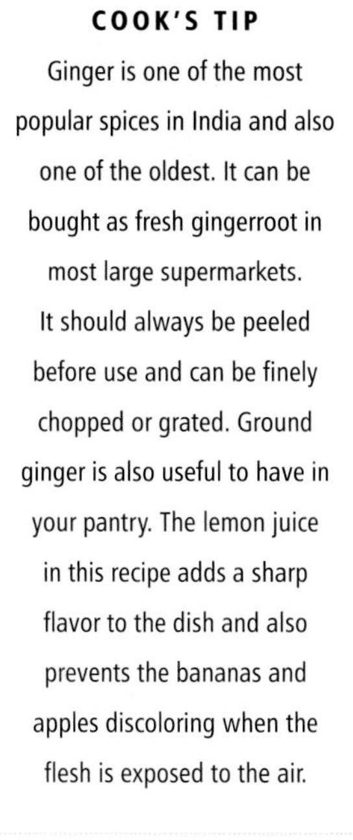

COOK'S TIP

Ginger is one of the most popular spices in India and also one of the oldest. It can be bought as fresh gingerroot in most large supermarkets. It should always be peeled before use and can be finely chopped or grated. Ground ginger is also useful to have in your pantry. The lemon juice in this recipe adds a sharp flavor to the dish and also prevents the bananas and apples discoloring when the flesh is exposed to the air.

1 Drain the fruit cocktail and place the fruit in a deep mixing bowl.

2 Mix the guavas and their syrup with the drained fruit cocktail.

3 Peel the bananas and cut into slices. Core and dice the apples.

4 Add the fresh fruit to the bowl containing the canned fruit and mix together.

5 Add the pepper, salt, lemon juice, and ginger and stir to mix.

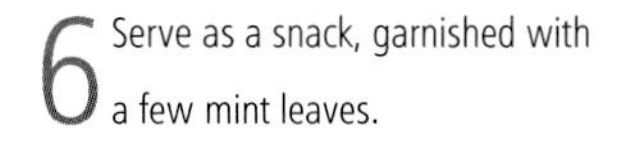

6 Serve as a snack, garnished with a few mint leaves.

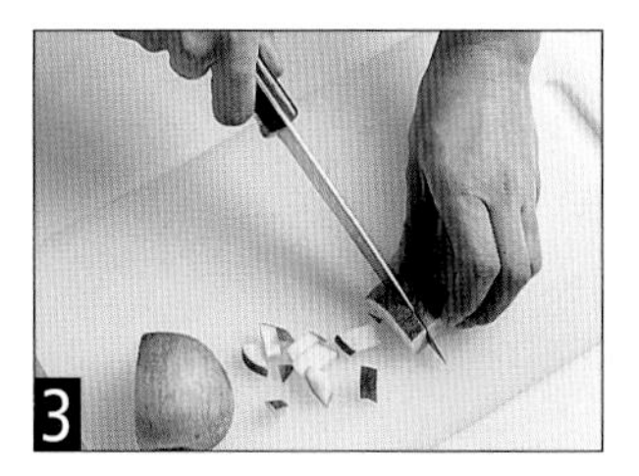

onion kachumbar

serves four

2 red onions or 1 Spanish onion, thinly sliced
1 fresh green chili, seeded and chopped
1 tbsp lime juice
¼ tsp chili powder
1 tbsp chopped cilantro
salt

1 Place the onion slices in a large serving bowl. Sprinkle with the chopped chili, lime juice, chili powder, cilantro, and salt to taste.

2 Toss well to coat the onion slices in the flavorings. Cover the bowl with plastic wrap.

3 Let stand in a cool place, but not the refrigerator, for 30 minutes, to enable the onion to release its juices. Toss the mixture again and taste and adjust the seasoning, if necessary, before serving.

COOK'S TIP

Red and Spanish onions are much sweeter than brown onions and are, therefore, a better choice for serving raw in this salad. No Indian meal is complete without an appetizing collection of small side dishes, which invariably include a simple salad. This one is the perfect foil for tandoori dishes and kabobs.

mixed rice, nuts & raisins

serves four

- scant ¼ cup chana dal
- 1¼ cups vegetable oil
- 2 tsp onion seeds
- 6 curry leaves
- 7 oz/200 g parva (flaked rice)
- 2 tbsp peanuts
- scant ¼ cup raisins
- generous ⅓ cup sugar
- 2 tsp salt
- 2 tsp chili powder
- 2 oz/55 g sev (optional)

1 Rinse the dal under cold running water, removing any stones. Soak in a bowl of water for at least 3 hours.

2 Heat the oil in a pan. Add the onion seeds and curry leaves and cook, stirring constantly, until the onion seeds are crisp and golden.

3 Add the parva (flaked rice) to the mixture in the pan and cook until crisp and golden (do not let it burn).

4 Remove the mixture from the pan and let drain on paper towels so that any excess oil is soaked up. Transfer to a bowl.

5 Cook the peanuts in the remaining oil, stirring constantly. Add the peanuts to the flaked rice mixture, stirring to mix well. Add the raisins, sugar, salt, and chili powder and mix together. Mix in the sev (if using). Transfer to a serving dish.

6 Reheat the oil remaining in the pan and cook the drained dal until golden. Add to the other ingredients in the serving dish and mix together.

7 This dish can be eaten straightaway or stored in an airtight container until you need it.

2

COOK'S TIP

Sev are very thin sticks made of besan and can be bought in Asian food stores.

3

5

shrimp sambal

serves four

9 oz/250 g cooked peeled shrimp, chopped
3 hard-cooked eggs, shelled and sliced
1 large onion, finely chopped
1¼-inch/3-cm piece fresh gingerroot, finely chopped
½ tsp chili powder
3 tbsp canned coconut milk
salt
½ tsp cumin seeds
TO GARNISH
1 lime, cut into wedges
cilantro sprigs

COOK'S TIP

If you shell the eggs immediately after hard-cooking them, you can avoid any discoloration around the yolk. To cool the cooked eggs quickly, rinse them under cold running water.

1 Place the shrimp, hard-cooked eggs, onion, ginger, chili powder, and coconut milk in a serving bowl and mix well. Season with salt to taste.

2 Place the cumin seeds in a mortar and lightly crush with a pestle.

3 Sprinkle the crushed cumin seeds over the sambal, then cover with plastic wrap and let chill in the refrigerator for at least 30 minutes. Serve garnished with lime wedges and cilantro sprigs.

chickpea salad

serves four

- 1½ cups canned chickpeas
- 4 carrots
- 1 bunch of scallions
- 1 cucumber
- ½ tsp salt
- ½ tsp pepper
- 3 tbsp lemon juice
- 1 red bell pepper, seeded and thinly sliced

1 Drain the chickpeas and place them in a large salad bowl.

2 Using a sharp knife, peel and slice the carrots. Cut the scallions into thin strips. Slice the cucumber, then cut into thick fourths. Add the carrots, scallions, and cucumber to the chickpeas and mix.

3 Stir in the salt and pepper and sprinkle with the lemon juice.

4 Gently toss the salad ingredients together using 2 serving spoons.

5 Using a sharp knife, slice the red bell pepper thinly.

6 Arrange the slices of red bell pepper on top of the chickpea salad. Serve the salad immediately or let chill in the refrigerator and serve when required.

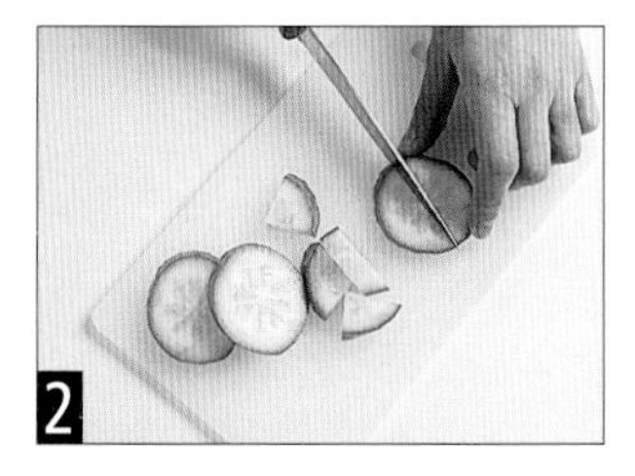

COOK'S TIP

Using canned chickpeas rather than the dried ones speeds up the cooking time.

eggplant purée

serves six

2 large eggplants, halved lengthwise
3 tbsp chopped cilantro
2 tsp ground coriander
1 tsp ground cumin
1 tsp ground turmeric
4 tomatoes, finely chopped
4 tbsp ghee or vegetable oil
1 onion, finely chopped
1 tsp Ginger Paste (see page 7)
1 tsp Garlic Paste (see page 7)
1 fresh green chili, finely chopped
salt
2 tbsp lemon juice
1 fresh mint sprig, to garnish
Chapatis (see page 185), to serve

1 Preheat the oven to 350°F/180°C. Place the eggplants, cut-sides up, in a shallow, ovenproof dish, then cover with foil and bake for 1 hour, or until the flesh is very soft. Let cool.

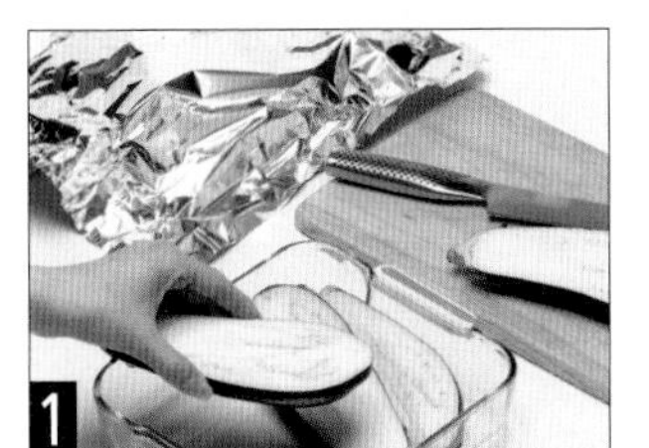

2 Scoop the eggplant flesh into a bowl and mash well. Beat in the cilantro, ground coriander, cumin, turmeric, and tomatoes with a wooden spoon.

3 Heat the ghee in a heavy-bottom skillet. Add the onion and cook over low heat, stirring occasionally, for 5 minutes, or until softened. Stir in the Ginger Paste, Garlic Paste, and chili and cook, stirring constantly, for 2 minutes. Add the eggplant mixture, then season with salt to taste and cook, stirring frequently, until the liquid has evaporated and the purée is thickened and fairly smooth. Sprinkle with the lemon juice, then spoon into a warmed serving bowl and garnish with a mint sprig. Serve immediately with Chapatis.

COOK'S TIP

Before baking the eggplants in the oven, use a sharp knife to slash the flesh of each half 2 or 3 times.

lime pickle

serves four

- 12 limes, halved and seeded
- 4 oz/115 g salt
- scant ½ cup chili powder
- 2 tbsp mustard powder
- 2 tbsp ground fenugreek
- 1 tbsp ground turmeric
- 1¼ cups mustard oil
- ½ oz/15 g yellow mustard seeds, crushed
- ½ tsp asafetida

COOK'S TIP

If you are absolutely certain that the jar won't crack when you add the hot oil in Step 3, then there is no need to transfer the lime mixture to a bowl to cool.

1 Cut each lime half into 4 pieces and pack them into a large, sterilized jar (see Cook's Tip, page 223), sprinkling over the salt at the same time. Cover and let stand in a warm place for 10–14 days, or until the limes have turned brown and softened.

2 Mix the chili powder, mustard powder, fenugreek, and turmeric together in a small bowl and add to the jar of limes. Stir to mix, then re-cover and let stand for 2 days.

3 Transfer the lime mixture to a heatproof bowl. Heat the oil in a heavy-bottom skillet. Add the mustard seeds and asafetida and cook, stirring constantly, until the oil is very hot and just beginning to smoke. Pour the oil and spices over the limes and mix well. Cover and let cool. When cool, pack into a sterilized jar and seal, then store in a sunny place for 1 week before serving.

raitas

serves four

MINT RAITA

generous ¾ cup plain yogurt

4 tbsp water

1 small onion, finely chopped

½ tsp mint sauce

½ tsp salt

3 fresh mint leaves, to garnish

CUCUMBER RAITA

8 oz/225 g cucumber

1 onion

½ tsp salt

½ tsp mint sauce

1¼ cup plain yogurt

⅔ cup water

fresh mint leaves, to garnish

EGGPLANT RAITA

1 eggplant

1 tsp salt

1 small onion, finely chopped

2 fresh green chilies, finely chopped

generous ¾ cup plain yogurt

3 tbsp water

1 To make the mint raita, place the yogurt in a bowl and whisk with a fork. Gradually add the water, whisking well. Add the onion, mint sauce, and salt and blend together. Garnish with the fresh mint leaves.

2 To make the cucumber raita, peel and slice the cucumber. Using a sharp knife, chop the onion finely. Place the cucumber and onion in a large bowl, then add the salt and the mint sauce. Add the yogurt and the water, place the mixture in a blender and blend well. Transfer to a serving bowl and serve garnished with a few fresh mint leaves.

3 To make the eggplant raita, rinse the eggplant and remove the top end. Discard the top and chop the rest into small pieces. Boil the eggplant in a pan of water until soft and mushy. Drain the eggplant and mash. Transfer to a serving bowl and add the salt, the onion, and chilies, mixing well. Whisk the yogurt with the water in a separate bowl and pour over the eggplant mixture. Mix well and serve.

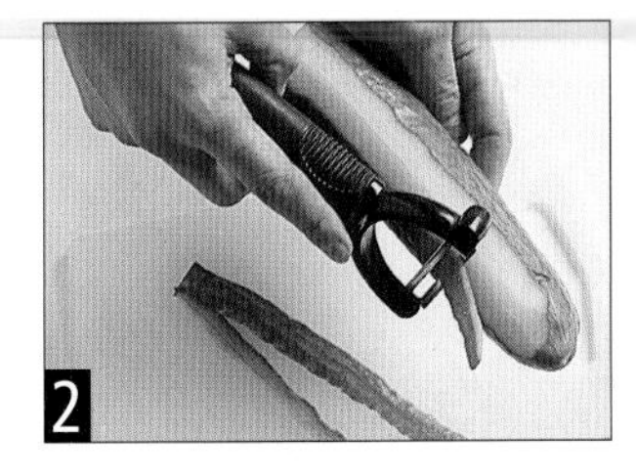

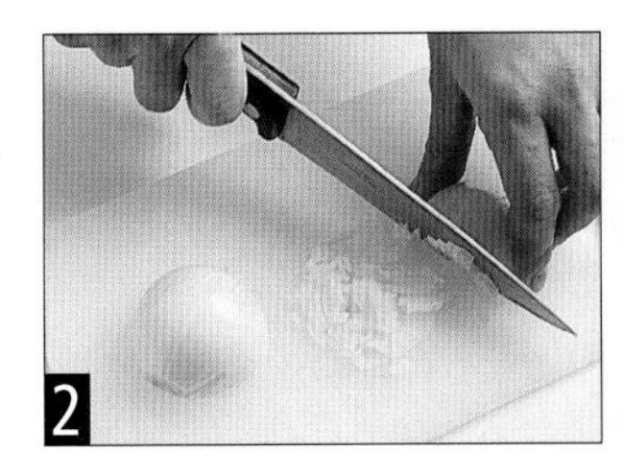

nine jewels chutney

serves four

- 1 tsp coriander seeds
- ½ tsp cumin seeds
- ½ tsp onion seeds
- ½ tsp aniseed
- ⅓ cup almonds, chopped
- 1 ripe mango, peeled, pitted, and sliced
- 1 eating apple, cored and chopped
- 1 banana, peeled and sliced
- 4 fresh pineapple slices, chopped or 4 canned pineapple slices in juice, drained, and chopped
- 8 oz/225 g canned peaches in fruit juice, drained and chopped
- ⅔ cup dried dates, pitted and sliced
- generous ⅓ cup raisins
- 2 dried red chilies
- 1½ oz/40 g piece fresh gingerroot, chopped
- 1 cup raw or muscovado sugar
- ¾ cup white wine or malt vinegar
- salt

1 Heat a heavy-bottom skillet. Add the coriander seeds, cumin seeds, onion seeds, aniseed, and almonds and cook over low heat, stirring constantly, for 1–2 minutes, or until the spices give off their aroma. Remove the skillet from the heat and reserve.

2 Place the mango, apple, banana, pineapple, peaches, dates, raisins, chilies, ginger, and sugar in a heavy-bottom pan. Pour in the vinegar, then add a pinch of salt and bring to a boil, stirring constantly. Reduce the heat and simmer gently, stirring frequently, for 15 minutes, or until thickened.

3 Stir in the spice mixture and cook, stirring frequently, for an additional 5 minutes. Remove from the heat and let cool. Either serve immediately or ladle into a sterilized jar (see Cook's Tip) and seal.

COOK'S TIP

To sterilize jars, boil clean jars in a pan of water for 10 minutes. Transfer to a preheated oven, 275°F/140°C, place upside down and dry for 15 minutes.

sesame seed chutney

serves four

- 8 tbsp sesame seeds
- 2 tbsp water
- ½ bunch of cilantro, finely chopped
- 3 fresh green chilies, chopped
- 1 tsp salt
- 2 tsp lemon juice
- 1 fresh red chili, chopped, to garnish

COOK'S TIP

Dry-roasting coaxes all of the flavor out of dried spices and gives dishes well-harmonized flavors that do not taste raw. Dry-roasting only takes a few minutes and you will be able to tell when the spices are ready because of the wonderful aroma they release. Be sure to stir the spices constantly and never take your eyes off the pan, because the spices can burn very quickly.

1 Place the sesame seeds in a large, heavy-bottom pan and dry-roast them. Remove the pan from the heat and let cool.

2 Once cooled, place the sesame seeds in a mortar or food processor and grind to form a fine powder. Add the water to the sesame seeds and mix to form a smooth paste.

3 Finely chop the cilantro and add to the sesame seeds with the chilies. Grind once again.

4 Add the salt and lemon juice to the mixture and grind again.

5 Remove the mixture from the food processor or mortar. Transfer to a serving dish and garnish with chopped chili. Serve.

mango chutney

serves four

2 lb 4 oz/1 kg fresh mangoes

4 tbsp salt

2½ cups water

2½ cups sugar

1¾ cups vinegar

2 tsp finely chopped fresh gingerroot

2 garlic cloves, crushed

2 tsp chili powder

2 cinnamon sticks

scant ½ cup raisins

generous ½ cup dates, pitted

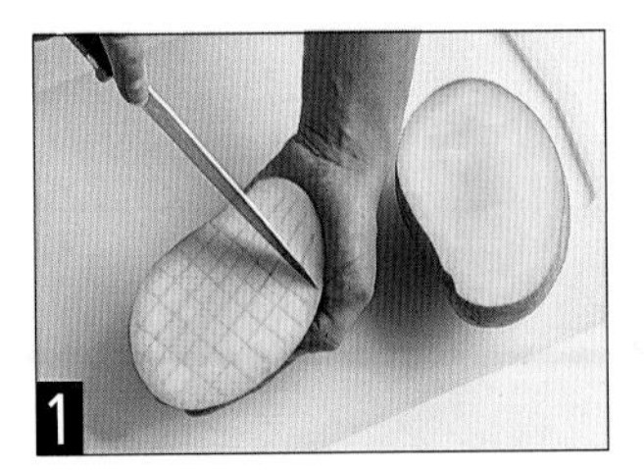

1 Using a sharp knife, halve and pit the mangoes—cut down on either side of the large pit and score the flesh, then turn inside out and cut off the mango cubes. Place the mango in a large bowl. Add the salt and water and let stand overnight. Drain the liquid from the mangoes and reserve.

2 Bring the sugar and vinegar to a boil in a large pan over low heat, stirring. Gradually add the mango cubes to the sugar and vinegar mixture, stirring to coat the mango in the mixture.

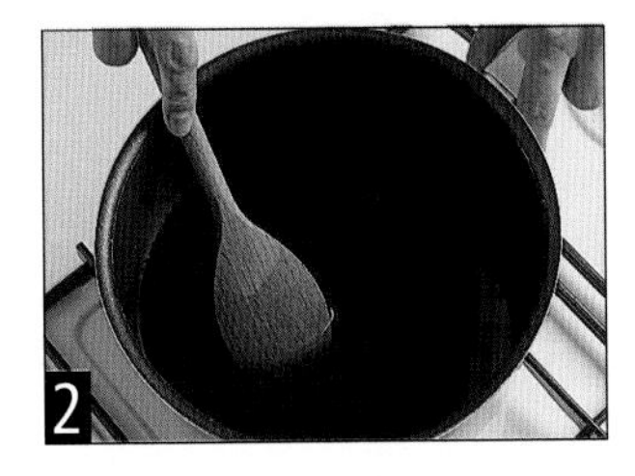

3 Add the ginger, garlic, chili powder, cinnamon sticks, raisins, and dates, and bring to a boil again, stirring occasionally. Reduce the heat and cook for 1 hour, or until the mixture thickens. Remove from the heat and let cool. Remove the cinnamon sticks and discard. Spoon the chutney into clean dry jars and cover tightly with lids. Let stand in a cool place so the flavors can fully develop.

COOK'S TIP

When choosing mangoes, select ones that are shiny with unblemished skins. To test if they are ripe, gently cup the mango in your hand and squeeze it gently—it should give slightly to the touch if ready for eating.

tamarind chutney

serves four–six

2 tbsp tamarind paste

5 tbsp water

1 tsp chili powder

½ tsp ground ginger

½ tsp salt

1 tsp sugar

1–2 tbsp finely chopped cilantro, to garnish

COOK'S TIP

Vegetable dishes are often given a sharp, sour flavor with the addition of tamarind. This is made from the semidried, compressed pulp of the tamarind tree. You can buy bars of the pungent-smelling pulp in Asian food stores. Store it in a tightly sealed plastic bag or airtight container. Alternatively, for greater convenience, keep a jar of tamarind paste in your pantry and use as required. Although tamarind is much more sour than lemon, lemon is often used as a substitute.

1 Place the tamarind paste in a small bowl.

2 Gradually add the water to the tamarind paste, gently whisking with a fork to form a smooth, runny consistency.

3 Add the chili powder and the ginger to the mixture and blend well.

4 Add the salt and the sugar and mix well.

5 Transfer the chutney to a serving dish and garnish with chopped cilantro. Serve.

Desserts

Indian desserts are quite rich and very sweet, so it is an excellent idea to offer a wide variety of fresh fruit—mangoes, guavas, or melon, for example—as well. These are best served chilled, especially in the summer months.

This chapter offers simple, everyday desserts, such as Indian Rice Pudding (see page 247), as well as more exotic creations. Among Indian people, some desserts such as Indian Bread Pudding (see page 230), Carrot Dessert (see page 235), and Indian Vermicelli Pudding (see page 251) are served only on special occasions, such as religious festivals. Few Indian restaurants in the West offer much in the way of special Indian desserts, so these recipes will come as a pleasant—and mouthwatering—surprise.

indian bread pudding

serves four–six

6 slices medium-sliced bread
5 tbsp ghee
10 tbsp sugar
1¼ cups water
3 green cardamoms, husks removed and seeds crushed
2½ cups milk
¾ cup evaporated milk or khoya (see Cook's Tip)
½ tsp saffron threads
cream, to serve (optional)

TO DECORATE
8 pistachio nuts, soaked, peeled and chopped
chopped almonds
2 varak (silver leaf) (optional)

COOK'S TIP

To make khoya, first bring 3¾ cups milk to a boil in a large, heavy-bottom pan, watching the milk carefully so that it doesn't burn. Reduce the heat and boil for 35 minutes, stirring occasionally.

1 Cut the slices of bread into fourths.

2

2 Heat the ghee in a skillet. Add the bread slices and cook, turning once, until a crisp golden brown color.

3 Place the fried bread in the bottom of a heatproof dish and reserve.

4

4 To make a syrup, place the sugar, water, and cardamom seeds in a pan and bring to a boil until the syrup thickens.

5 Pour the syrup over the fried bread in the dish.

6

6 Place the milk, evaporated milk, and saffron in a separate pan and bring to a boil over low heat until the milk has halved in volume.

7 Pour the milk over the syrup-coated bread.

8 Decorate with the pistachios, chopped almonds, and varak (if using). Serve the bread pudding with or without cream.

coconut sweet

serves four–six

¾ stick butter

2 cups dry unsweetened coconut

¾ cup condensed milk

few drops pink food coloring (optional)

1 Place the butter in a heavy-bottom pan and melt over low heat, stirring constantly.

2 Add the dry unsweetened coconut to the melted butter, stirring to mix.

3 Stir in the condensed milk and the pink food coloring (if using) and mix constantly for 7–10 minutes.

4 Remove the pan from the heat and let the coconut mixture cool slightly.

5 Once cool enough to handle, shape the coconut mixture into long blocks and cut into equal-size rectangles. Let set for 1 hour, then serve.

VARIATION

If you prefer, you could divide the coconut mixture in two, and add the pink food coloring to only one half of the mixture. This way, you will have an attractive combination of pink and white coconut sweets.

COOK'S TIP

Coconut is used extensively in Indian cooking to add flavor and creaminess to various dishes. The best flavor comes from freshly grated coconut, although ready-prepared dry unsweetened coconut, as used here, makes an excellent standby. Freshly grated coconut freezes successfully, so it is well worth preparing when you have the time.

almond slices

serves six–eight

- 3 eggs
- ¾ cup ground almonds
- 2½ cups milk powder
- 1 cup sugar
- ½ tsp saffron threads
- scant 1 stick unsalted butter
- ¼ cup slivered almonds

1 Preheat the oven to 325°F/160°C. Beat the eggs together in a bowl and reserve until required.

2 Place the ground almonds, milk powder, sugar, and saffron in a large bowl and stir to mix well.

2

4

5

3 Melt the butter in a small pan.

COOK'S TIP

These almond slices are best eaten hot, but they may also be served cold. They can be made a day or even a week in advance and reheated. They also freeze beautifully.

4 Pour the melted butter over the dry ingredients and mix well with a wooden spoon.

5 Add the reserved beaten eggs to the mixture and stir to blend well.

6 Spread the mixture in a shallow 6–8-inch/15–20-cm square ovenproof dish and bake in the preheated oven for 45 minutes. Test whether the cake is cooked through by piercing with the tip of a knife or a skewer—it will come out clean if it is cooked thoroughly.

7 Using a sharp knife, cut the almond cake into slices.

8 Decorate the almond slices with slivered almonds and transfer to a serving dish. Serve hot or cold.

almond & pistachio dessert

serves four–six

scant ¾ stick unsalted butter

2 cups ground almonds

1 cup sugar

⅔ cup light cream

8 almonds, chopped

10 pistachio nuts, chopped

1 Melt the butter in a medium-size, preferably nonstick pan, stirring well.

2 Add the ground almonds, sugar, and cream to the melted butter in the pan, stirring well. Reduce the heat and stir constantly for 10–12 minutes, scraping the base of the pan.

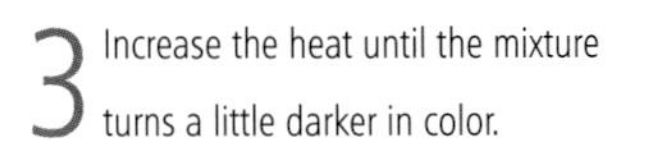

3 Increase the heat until the mixture turns a little darker in color.

4 Transfer the almond mixture to a shallow serving dish and smooth the top with the back of a spoon.

5 Decorate the dessert with the chopped almonds and pistachios.

6 Leave the dessert to set for 1 hour, then cut into diamond shapes and serve cold.

COOK'S TIP

You could use a variety of shaped cookie cutters to cut the dessert into different shapes, rather than diamonds, if you prefer. This almond dessert can be made in advance and stored in an airtight container in the refrigerator for several days.

carrot dessert

serves four–six

3 lb 5 oz/1.5 kg carrots

10 tbsp pure ghee

2½ cups milk

¾ cup evaporated milk or khoya
(see Cook's Tip, page 230)

10 cardamoms, husks removed and
seeds crushed

8–10 tbsp sugar

TO DECORATE

scant ¼ cup pistachio nuts, chopped

2 varak (silver leaf) (optional)

COOK'S TIP

This dessert tastes better made with pure ghee. However, if you are trying to limit your fat intake, use vegetable ghee instead. A quicker way to grate the carrots is to use a food processor.

1 Peel and grate the carrots, then reserve.

2 Heat the ghee in a large, heavy-bottom skillet.

3 Add the grated carrots and stir-fry for 15–20 minutes, or until the moisture from the carrots has evaporated and the carrots have darkened in color.

4 Add the milk, evaporated milk, cardamoms, and sugar to the carrot mixture and continue to stir for an additional 30–35 minutes, or until the mixture is a rich brownish-red color.

5 Transfer the carrot mixture to individual serving dishes.

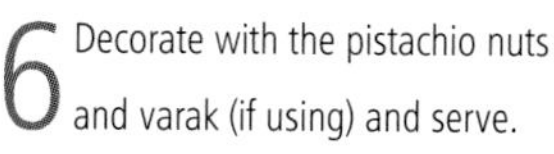

6 Decorate with the pistachio nuts and varak (if using) and serve.

sweet potato dessert

serves eight–ten

2 lb 4 oz/1 kg sweet potatoes

3¾ cups milk

generous ¾ cup sugar

few chopped almonds, to decorate

COOK'S TIP

Sweet potatoes are longer than ordinary potatoes and have a pinkish or yellowish skin with yellow or white flesh. As their name suggests, they taste slightly sweet.

1 Using a sharp knife, peel the sweet potatoes, then rinse under cold water and cut them into slices.

2 Place the sweet potato slices in a large pan. Cover with 2½ cups of the milk and cook slowly until the sweet potato is soft enough to be mashed.

3 Remove the pan from the heat and mash the sweet potatoes with a potato masher to remove all the lumps.

4 Add the sugar and remaining milk to the mashed sweet potatoes, and carefully stir to blend together.

5 Return the pan to the heat and let the mixture simmer until it begins to thicken (it should reach the consistency of a cream of chicken soup).

6 Transfer the sweet potato dessert to a serving dish.

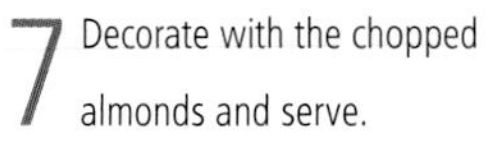

7 Decorate with the chopped almonds and serve.

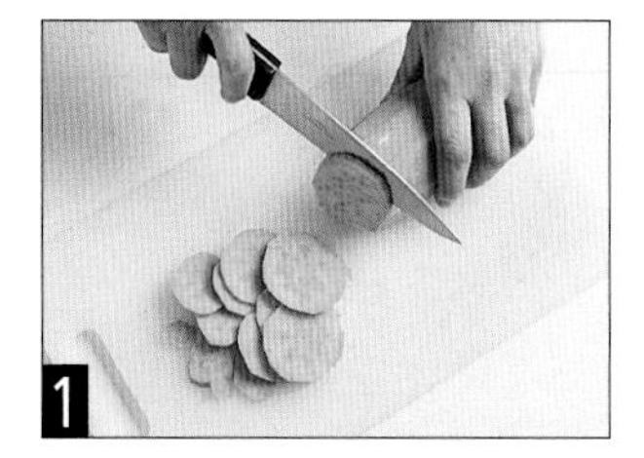

sweet saffron rice

serves four

1 cup basmati rice
1 cup sugar
pinch of saffron threads
1¼ cups water
2 tbsp ghee
3 cloves
3 cardamoms
scant ¼ cup golden raisins
TO DECORATE
few pistachio nuts (optional)
varak (silver leaf) (optional)

1 Rinse the rice twice under cold running water, then bring to a boil in a pan of water, stirring. Remove the pan from the heat when the rice is half cooked, then drain thoroughly and reserve.

2 Boil the sugar, saffron, and water together in a separate pan, stirring, until the syrup thickens. Reserve until required.

3 Heat the ghee, cloves, and cardamoms in a separate pan, stirring occasionally. Remove the pan from the heat.

4 Return the rice to low heat and add the golden raisins, stirring. Pour the syrup over the rice mixture and stir.

5 Pour the ghee mixture over the rice and let simmer over low heat for 10–15 minutes. Check to see whether the rice is cooked; if not, add a little water, then cover and let simmer. Serve warm, decorated with pistachio nuts and varak (silver leaf, if using).

VARIATION

For a stronger saffron flavor, place the saffron threads on a piece of foil and toast them lightly under a hot broiler for a few moments (take care not to burn them). Crush finely before adding to the sugar to make the syrup.

pooris stuffed with chana dal halva

serves four–six

generous 1 cup coarse semolina
⅔ cup all-purpose flour, plus extra for dusting
½ tsp salt
1½ tsp ghee
⅔ cup milk
FILLING
8 tbsp chana dal
3¾ cups water
5 tbsp ghee, plus extra for frying
2 green cardamoms, husks removed and seeds crushed
4 cloves
8 tbsp sugar
2 tbsp ground almonds
½ tsp saffron threads
scant ⅓ cup golden raisins

1 Place the semolina, flour, and salt in a bowl and mix. Add the ghee and rub it in with your fingers. Add the milk and mix to form a dough. Knead the dough for 5 minutes, then cover and let rise for about 3 hours. Knead the dough on a floured counter for 15 minutes.

2 Roll out the dough until it measures 10 inches/25 cm square and divide into 10 portions. Roll out each of these into 5-inch/13-cm circles and set aside. To make the filling, soak the dal for at least 3 hours, if time allows. Place the dal in a pan and add the water. Bring to a boil over medium heat until all of the water has evaporated and the dal is soft enough to be mashed into a paste.

3 Heat the ghee in a separate pan. Add the cardamom seeds and cloves and reduce the heat, then add the dal paste and stir for 5–7 minutes.

4 Fold in the sugar and almonds and cook, stirring, for 10 minutes. Add the saffron and golden raisins and blend until thickened, stirring, for 5 minutes. Spoon the filling onto one half of each pastry round. Dampen the edges with water and fold the other half over to seal.

5 Heat the ghee in a skillet. Add the pooris and cook over low heat until golden. Transfer the pooris to paper towels, then drain and serve.

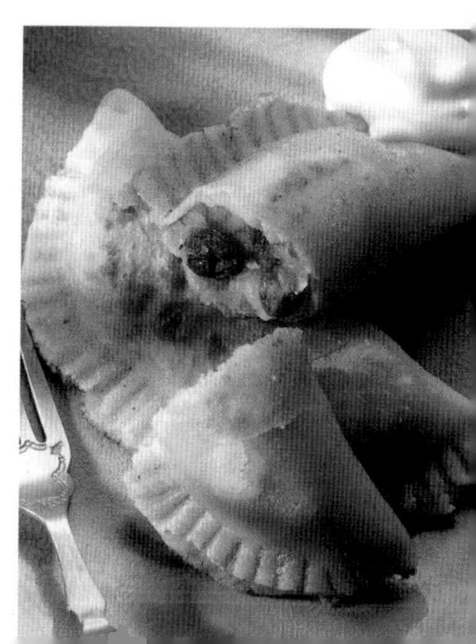

almond sherbet

serves two

2 cups whole almonds

2 tbsp sugar

1¼ cups milk

1¼ cups water

COOK'S TIP

An electric coffee grinder or spice mill will greatly cut down the time taken to grind the almonds. If using a coffee grinder that is also used for coffee, always remember to clean the grinder thoroughly afterward, otherwise you will end up with strange-tasting coffee! A pestle and mortar will take longer and is also not as good for large quantities.

In India, ice-cool sherbets such as this one are served on special occasions, such as religious festivals. They would be served on the very finest tableware and decorated with varak (edible silver leaf).

1 Soak the almonds in a bowl of water for at least 3 hours or preferably overnight.

2 Using a sharp knife, chop the almonds into small pieces. Grind to a fine paste in a food processor or using a pestle and mortar.

3 Add the sugar to the almond paste and grind once again to form a fine paste.

4 Add the milk and water and mix well (in a blender if you have one).

5 Transfer the almond sherbet to a large serving dish.

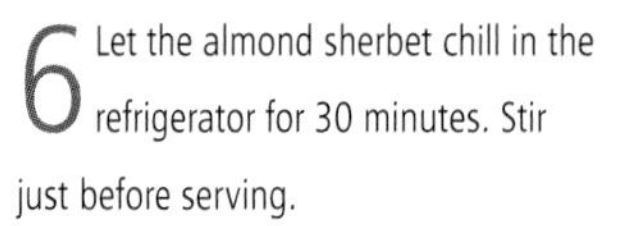

6 Let the almond sherbet chill in the refrigerator for 30 minutes. Stir just before serving.

pistachio dessert

serves four–six

3¾ cups water
1⅔ cups pistachio nuts
3 cups whole milk powder
2¼ cups sugar
2 cardamoms, husks removed and seeds crushed
2 tbsp rose water
few saffron threads

TO DECORATE

¼ cup slivered almonds
fresh mint leaves

1 Boil 2½ cups of the water in a pan. Remove the pan from the heat and soak the pistachio nuts in this water for 5 minutes. Drain the pistachio nuts thoroughly and remove the skins.

2 Grind the pistachio nuts in a food processor or use a pestle and mortar.

3 Add the dried milk powder to the ground pistachio nuts and mix well.

COOK'S TIP

It is best to buy whole pistachio nuts and grind them yourself, rather than using packets of ready-ground nuts. Freshly ground nuts have the best flavor, as grinding releases their natural oils.

4 To make the syrup, place the remaining water and the sugar in a pan and heat gently. When the liquid begins to thicken, add the cardamom seeds, rose water, and saffron.

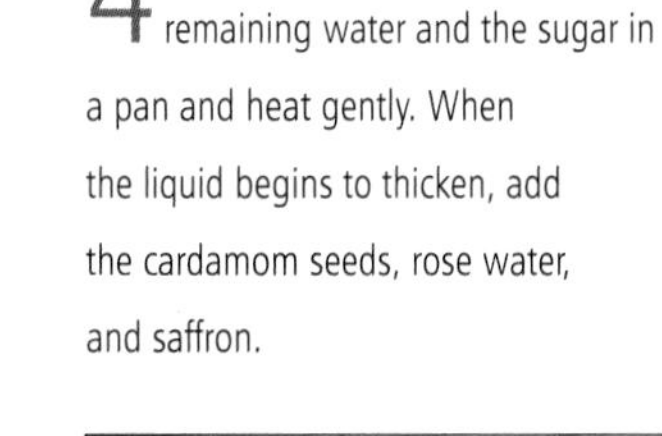

5 Add the syrup to the pistachio mixture and cook for 5 minutes, stirring, until the mixture thickens. Let the mixture cool slightly.

6 Once cooled enough to handle, roll the pistachio mixture into balls. Decorate with the slivered almonds and mint leaves and let set before serving.

deep-fried sweetmeats in syrup

serves six–eight

5 tbsp whole milk powder
1½ tbsp all-purpose flour
1 tsp baking powder
1½ tbsp unsalted butter
1 egg
1 tsp milk to mix (if required)
10 tbsp ghee

SYRUP
3 cups water
8 tbsp sugar
2 green cardamoms, with husks removed and seeds crushed
large pinch of saffron threads
2 tbsp rose water

1 Place the milk powder, flour, and baking powder in a bowl.

2 Place the butter in a pan and heat until melted, stirring.

3 Whisk the egg in a bowl. Add the melted butter and whisked egg to the dry ingredients and blend together (add the teaspoon of milk at this stage, if necessary) to form a soft dough.

3

4 Break the dough into 12 small pieces and shape, in the palms of your hands, into small, smooth balls.

4

5 Heat the ghee in a deep skillet. Reduce the heat and then start cooking the dough balls, 3–4 at a time, tossing and turning gently with a slotted spoon until a dark golden brown color. Remove the sweetmeats from the pan and let stand in a deep serving bowl.

6 To make the syrup, boil the water and sugar in a pan for 7–10 minutes. Add the crushed cardamom seeds and saffron, and pour over the sweetmeats.

6

7 Pour the rose water sparingly over the top. Let soak for 10 minutes for the sweetmeats to absorb plenty of the syrup. Serve the sweetmeats hot or cold.

ground almonds cooked in ghee & milk

serves two–four

2 tbsp ghee

2 tbsp all-purpose flour

generous 1 cup ground almonds

1¼ cups milk

scant ¼ cup sugar

fresh mint leaves, to decorate

COOK'S TIP

Ghee comes in two forms and can be bought from Asian food stores. It is worth noting that pure ghee, made from melted butter, is not suitable for vegans, although there is a vegetable ghee available from specialty Asian food stores and some healthfood stores.

1 Place the ghee in a small, heavy-bottom pan. Melt the ghee over low heat, stirring so that it does not burn.

2 Reduce the heat and add the flour, stirring vigorously to remove any lumps.

2

3

4

3 Add the almonds to the ghee and flour mixture, stirring constantly.

4 Gradually add the milk and sugar to the mixture in the pan and bring to a boil. Continue cooking for 3–5 minutes, or until the liquid is smooth and reaches the consistency of cream of chicken soup.

5 Transfer to a serving dish, decorate with mint leaves and serve hot.

VARIATION

You could use coconut milk in this recipe, for a delicious alternative.

fruit & nut ice cream

serves six

5 cups canned evaporated milk, unopened
3 egg whites
3 cups confectioners' sugar
generous 1¼ cups chopped pistachio nuts, plus extra to decorate
¾ cup slivered almonds
scant ¼ cup candied cherries, coarsely chopped, plus extra to decorate
½ cup golden raisins
1 tsp ground cardamom

1 Begin preparing the day before you want to serve the ice cream. Place the cans of evaporated milk on their sides in a large, heavy-bottom pan. Pour in enough water to come about three-quarters of the way up their sides and bring to a boil. Reduce the heat, then cover tightly and simmer for 20 minutes. Remove from the heat and let cool, then chill for 24 hours. Place a large bowl in the refrigerator to chill.

2 The next day, whisk the egg whites in a spotlessly clean, greasefree bowl until soft peaks form. Pour the evaporated milk into the chilled bowl and whisk until doubled in size. Fold in the egg whites, then the sugar. Gently fold in the pistachio nuts, almonds, cherries, golden raisins, and ground cardamom.

COOK'S TIP

Don't forget to remove the labels from the cans before boiling the evaporated milk.

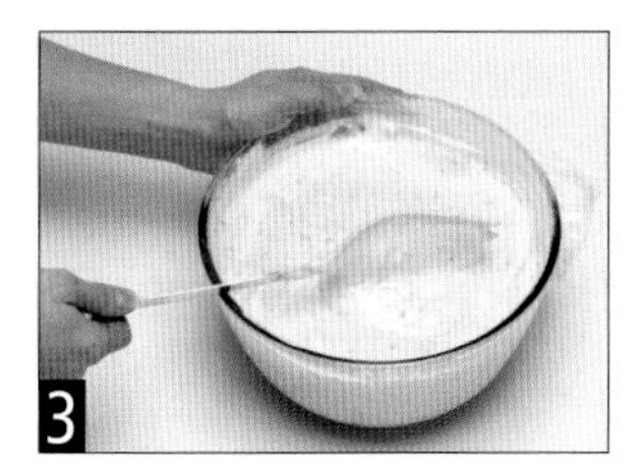

3 Cover the bowl with plastic wrap and freeze for 1 hour. Remove the bowl from the freezer and beat the mixture. Spoon into a freezerproof container and freeze for 3 hours or preferably overnight, until set.

4 Scoop the ice cream into dishes. Decorate with chopped pistachio nuts and candied cherries and serve.

rice pudding

serves eight–ten

- generous ⅓ cup basmati rice
- 5 cups milk
- 8 tbsp sugar
- varak (silver leaf) or chopped pistachio nuts, to decorate
- Pooris (see page 184), to serve

COOK'S TIP

Varak (varaq, vark) is edible silver leaf that is used in India to decorate elaborate dishes prepared for the most special occasions and celebrations, such as weddings. It is pure silver that has been beaten until it is wafer-thin. It comes with a piece of backing paper which is peeled off as the varak is laid on the cooked food. It is extremely delicate and so must be handled with care. You can buy varak from Asian food stores. Remember that because it is pure silver it should be stored in an airtight bag or box to avoid tarnishing.

1 Rinse the rice and place in a large pan. Add 2½ cups of the milk and bring to a boil over very low heat. Cook until the milk has been completely absorbed by the rice, stirring occasionally.

2 Remove the pan from the heat. Mash the rice, making swift, round movements in the pan, for at least 5 minutes, until all of the lumps have been removed.

VARIATION

If you prefer, you can substitute American or Patna long-grain rice for the basmati rice.

3 Return the pan to the heat and gradually add the remaining milk. Bring to a boil over low heat, stirring occasionally.

4 Add the sugar and continue to cook, stirring constantly, for 7–10 minutes or until the mixture is quite thick in consistency.

5 Transfer the rice pudding to a heatproof serving bowl. Decorate with varak (silver leaf) or chopped pistachio nuts and serve on its own or with Pooris.

semolina dessert

serves four

6 tbsp ghee
3 cloves
3 cardamoms
8 tbsp coarse semolina
½ tsp saffron threads
scant ⅓ cup golden raisins
10 tbsp sugar
1¼ cups water
1¼ cups milk
cream, to serve
TO DECORATE
scant ⅓ cup dry unsweetened coconut, toasted
scant ¼ cup chopped almonds
scant ¼ cup pistachio nuts, soaked and chopped (optional)

1 Place the ghee in a pan and melt over medium heat.

2 Add the cloves and cardamoms to the melted butter and reduce the heat, stirring to mix. Add the semolina and stir until it turns a shade darker.

3 Add the saffron, golden raisins, and sugar to the mixture, stirring to mix well.

2

2

3

4 Pour in the water and milk and stir the mixture constantly until the semolina has softened. Add more water if it becomes too solid.

5 Remove the pan from the heat and transfer the semolina to a serving dish.

6 Decorate the semolina dessert with the toasted dry unsweetened coconut, chopped almonds, and pistachio nuts (if using). Serve with a little cream drizzled over the top.

COOK'S TIP

Cloves are used to give flavor and aroma to both sweet and savory dishes. They should be used with caution because the flavor can be overwhelming if too many are used, and should be removed before the dish is served.

mango ice cream

serves six

- 2/3 cup heavy cream
- 2 tbsp superfine sugar
- generous 1 3/4 cups mango juice
- 1/2 tsp ground cinnamon
- slivered almonds, to decorate

COOK'S TIP

Don't beat the cream too vigorously—only whisk it enough to make a smooth mixture and to dissolve the sugar.

1 Pour the cream into a large bowl, then add the sugar and whisk lightly until dissolved. Stir in the mango juice and cinnamon.

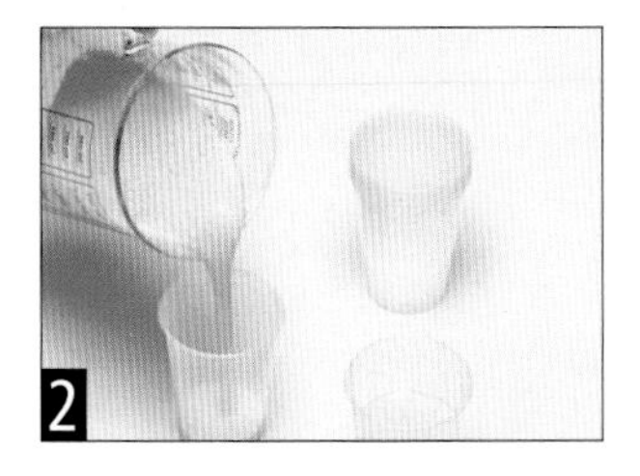

2 Pour the mixture into 6 freezerproof molds and cover with foil, then place in the freezer for 3 hours or preferably overnight, until set. During the first hour of freezing, gently shake the molds 3 times.

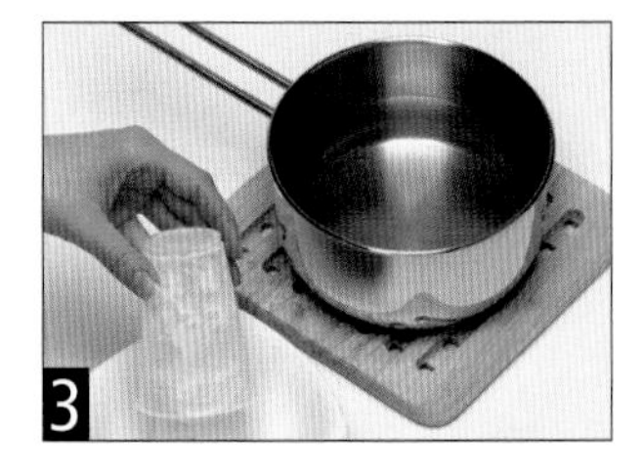

3 To serve, dip the bases of the molds in hot water, then invert onto individual serving plates. Decorate with slivered almonds and serve immediately.

indian vermicelli pudding

serves four–six

scant ¼ cup pistachio nuts (optional)

¼ cup slivered almonds

3 tbsp ghee

3½ oz/100 g seviyan
(Indian vermicelli)

3¾ cups milk

¾ cup evaporated milk

8 tbsp sugar

6 dates, pitted

1 Soak the pistachio nuts (if using) in a bowl of water for at least 3 hours. Peel the pistachios and mix them with the slivered almonds. Chop the nuts finely and reserve

COOK'S TIP

You can find seviyan (Indian vermicelli) in Asian food stores. This dessert can be served warm or cold.

2 Melt the ghee in a large pan and lightly fry the seviyan. Reduce the heat immediately (the seviyan will turn golden brown very quickly, so be careful not to burn it), and if necessary remove the pan from the heat. Do not worry if some bits are a little darker than others.

3 Add the milk to the seviyan and bring to a boil slowly, taking care that it does not boil over.

4 Add the evaporated milk, sugar, and the pitted dates to the mixture in the pan. Let simmer for 10 minutes, uncovered, stirring occasionally. When the consistency begins to thicken, pour the pudding into a serving bowl.

5 Decorate the pudding with the prepared pistachio nuts and almonds and serve.

indian fruit & custard

serves six

- 1 tbsp blanched almonds
- 4 cups milk
- 1¾ cups evaporated milk
- 1 tbsp rose water
- 1 tsp ground cardamom
- a few drops of yellow food coloring (optional)
- fresh fruit, such as mango and papaya slices and mixed berries
- 1 tbsp pistachio nuts, chopped, to decorate (optional)

1 Dry-fry the almonds in a heavy-bottom pan over low heat, stirring constantly, for 1–2 minutes, or until golden. Remove the pan from the heat and reserve.

2 Bring the milk to a boil in a separate pan, then reduce the heat and simmer for 30 minutes, or until reduced by about half. Strain into a clean pan, then place over very low heat and stir in the evaporated milk, rose water, and cardamom. Add a few drops of food coloring to tint the custard an attractive golden yellow, if you like. Simmer gently, stirring frequently to prevent the custard catching on the base of the pan, for 15 minutes, or until thickened and smooth.

3 Pour the custard into a bowl and stir in the reserved almonds. Cover with plastic wrap and let cool, then chill in the refrigerator for at least 1 hour and up to 8 hours. Slice the fruit just before serving. Divide the custard between individual serving plates, arrange the fruit beside it and sprinkle with the pistachios (if using).

COOK'S TIP

Reducing milk as a basis for desserts is a popular technique in India. Evaporated milk also features in a number of favorite desserts.